Popular Day Hikes 1

Kananaskis Country

Gillean Daffern

Rocky
Mountain Books
Calgary–Victoria–Vancouver

Cover: Burstall Pass Trail just below the pass. In the background rises Mount Sir Douglas.
Title page: Indian Paintbrush

Copyright © 2007, 2008 Gillean Daffern
Reprinted 2010
All rights reserved. No part of this publication may be reproduced, stored in a retrieval system, or transmitted in any form or by any means—electronic, mechanical, audio recording, or otherwise—without the written permission of the publisher or a photocopying licence from Access Copyright, Toronto, Canada.

Rocky Mountain Books
#108 – 17665 66A Avenue
Surrey, BC V3S 2A7
www.rmbooks.com

Rocky Mountain Books
PO Box 468
Custer, WA
98240-0468

Library and Archives Canada Cataloguing in Publication

Daffern, Gillean, 1938-
      Popular day hikes : Kananaskis country / Gillean Daffern.
ISBN 978-1-894765-90-9

      1. Trails—Alberta—Kananaskis Country—Guidebooks. 2. Kananaskis Country (Alta.)—Guidebooks. 3. Hiking—Alberta—Kananaskis Country— Guidebooks. I. Title.

GV199.44.C22K36 2007   917.123'32043   C2006-906599-3

Library of Congress Control Number: 2006940300

Book design by Gillean Daffern
Cover design by Jacqui Thomas
Proofread by Corina Skavberg
All cover and interior photographs provided by Gillean Daffern unless otherwise noted.
Printed in China

Rocky Mountain Books acknowledges the financial support for its publishing program from the Government of Canada through the Book Publishing Industry Development Program (BPIDP), Canada Council for the Arts, and the province of British Columbia through the British Columbia Arts Council and the Book Publishing Tax Credit.

This book has been produced on 100% post-consumer recycled paper, processed chlorine free and printed with vegetable-based dyes.

Disclaimer

Introduction

About Kananaskis Country

Kananaskis Country (commonly called K Country) is located on the eastern slopes of the Canadian Rockies, west and south of the Olympic city of Calgary, Alberta.

In the west near the Great Divide the scenery is much the same as in the adjoining Banff National Park: High limestone peaks (up to 3449 m), glaciers, waterfalls, blue-green lakes, boisterous streams, forested valley bottoms of spruce and fir with larches at treeline. Winter snowfall can be heavy, so some trails, such as Burstall Pass trail, may not be clear of snow until mid July.

To the east the friendly foothills are a mosaic of sandstone bluffs, pine/aspen forests and meadows. They dry quickly of snow, making hiking possible from March to November, and sometimes right through the winter.

In between are the Front Ranges, a complex jumble of arid valleys, rocky peaks and interconnecting ridges built of both limestones and sandstones. It's here you'll find easy peaks to climb and ridges to wander over, the Centennial Trail being a prime example.

Alpine meadows are sandwiched between forest and rock and coat many good hiking ridges. For too brief a time from late June to mid August, they are crammed with flowers. In particular, overseas visitors will be intoxicated by the gaudy colours of North America's Indian Paintbrush. I advise all flower buffs to buy a field guide to put in the pack.

Getting there

See the map on page 6. Other than Greyhound buses that run along the Trans-Canada Highway between Calgary and Canmore, there is no public transportation. You need to rent a car. Consider also a mountain bike for some trails. Know that all the trails in this book are accessible from Calgary as a day trip.

Seasonal road closures

Hwy. 40 is closed December 1 to June 14 between Kananaskis Lakes Trail (road) and Highwood Junction.

Hwy. 66 is closed December 1 to May 14 west of Elbow Falls parking lot. Also closed December 1 to May 14 is Hwy. 546 west of Sandy McNabb Recreation Area, Powderface Trail between Dawson trailhead and Hwy. 66 and all of the Gorge Creek Trail.

Facilities

Calgary, Cochrane, Canmore, Bragg Creek, Turner Valley, Black Diamond and Longview have all the amenities.

Hwy. 1A Exshaw: Heart Mountain Store (cafe, groceries, gas).

Hwy. 1X Bow Valley Provincial Park: Small store at Bow Valley campground.

Hwy. 1 Dead Man's Flat: Motel, B&B, gas station/small grocery store, a few eateries. Rafter Six Ranch Resort: accommodation, camping, lounge, dining room, Sunday brunch. (Booking ahead for meals is appreciated. Same day is fine.)

Hwy. 40 Kananaskis Village and Ribbon Creek: two hotels, one hostel, small grocery store with snacks, outdoor rental store, numerous eateries and watering holes. Fortress Junction: Gas, good grocery selection and snack bar. Highwood Junction: Gas, some groceries and snacks. Sundance Lodges: camping in teepees, small store. Boundary Ranch: restaurant (hearty western-style). Kananaskis Country Golf Course: restaurant.

Kananaskis Lakes Trail Boulton Creek restaurant /grocery store.

Hwy. 742 Mount Engadine Lodge: accommodation (all meals provided), evening meals at 24 hours notice.

Hwy. 66—on nearby McLean Creek Trail (road)—McLean Creek Camper Centre: some groceries and snacks.

Weather

Snow can fall in any month of the year in the Canadian Rockies. Having said that, hiking usually starts in April in eastern K Country. In May there is usually a period of warm sunny weather. Rains fall mainly in June–the peak run-off time. During July and August temperatures can reach the mid 30s and any rain is often associated with late afternoon thunderstorms. Smoke haze from far off forest fires may bother some people. The weather starts cooling off in mid September. Indian summers can occur in late September through October and are glorious, bringing sunny stable weather. By late October and November temperatures are dipping to the minus 20s and snow that falls stays over the winter. But all is not lost. During this period chinook winds can roar in and raise the temperatures by 20 degrees in an hour. This occurs mainly in eastern K Country where is it sometimes possible to hike all the year round.

Generally, low cloud is not the problem it is in other wetter ranges of the world and navigating by compass in K Country is an unusual event.

Drinking Water

Most locals drink from the creeks. However, there is a chance the water, especially the water in the eastern foothills, may be contaminated by *Giardia lamblia*, a parasite that can cause severe gastrointestinal distress. It is best to carry water from your home, hotel or campground.

Wildlife Concerns

At all times be aware of bears, both Grizzly and Black bears, particularly in early fall when the berries ripen. It's a good idea to phone ahead and find out if there have been any sightings in the area you are going to. K Country will often close a trail until a bear has moved out of the area. Make a lot of noise if you suspect there is a bear in the area.

Elk and moose should also be given a wide berth, especially in fall during the mating season when males get very ornery. Lately, cougars have become a year round worry. However, they are rarely seen, as are wolves. Be wary of picas, ground squirrels and chipmunks. They bite and could carry disease.

Ticks are lurking about between about March and mid June in areas where there is a lot of sheep, such as Teahouse Ridge on Lady MacDonald. Wear light-coloured clothing—all the better to see them—and do a thorough check of your body and clothes BEFORE you get into your car! In this part of the Rockies, none of the ticks carry Lyme's Disease.

A few rules to know about

- No registration is necessary. However, for your safety, registration books are available at information centres.
- Respect trail closures, open fire bans.
- Dogs must be on a leash.

Safety Tips

- It is safer to travel with company. If you travel alone, let someone know where you are going and when you expect to return.
- Unless you are a seasoned hiker who knows the area well, going off trail can be fraught with dangers. Rock is usually friable and rockfall common.
- Start early, especially during the summer thunderstorm season. Carry a flashlight or headlamp when the days become shorter.
- Carry bear repellent and read up on what to do if you encounter a bear/cougar. K Country information centres carry leaflets on the subject.
- Hunting is allowed everywhere except in provincial parks and provincial recreation areas. September to November is the time to dress in red. Know that hunting is not allowed on Sundays.
- Carry a cellphone.

Using this book

How the trails were chosen

For their popularity, first of all. You are not likely to be alone. They are easily accessible from a road, start from parking lots that usually have biffies and picnic tables, have no major river crossings and are generally well-marked. To give variety they range from short to long and from easy walks to easy scrambles. Because of the constraints, this selection does not mean they are my favourite trails, or even that they are the best trails. See Doing More.

Trails

In this book, well-marked trails have signposts of the "You are here" variety at junctions, and coloured markers or arrows on trees and posts in between junctions. Above treeline watch for cairns, paint splodges or metal tags on rocks. Other trails, while not marked in any way apart from cairns or flagging are well used and obvious. Some trails are shared with mountain bikers and equestrians, most often those in the foothills.

Options

Type in blue indicates Going Farther, Detours and Optional Returns. A few of the Optional Returns require a second vehicle or a bicycle.

Numbers in Text

For clarity the text is written in short numbered paragraphs. Numbers in the photo captions refer back to the paragraph numbers. Numbers in photo captions with an O in front of them, refer to the option.

Difficulty

Describes conditions underfoot and the steepness of the grades. Scramble steps are noted. A few of the Going Farthers involve scrambling or going off trail.

Except after rain or during the runoff, minor creek crossings can usually be jumped or crossed on rocks. I mention whether creeks are bridged or not.

Distances

Distances are round trip, car to car.

Sketch Maps

Red lines indicate main trails. Red-dashed lines are options. Black-dashed lines are other trails and are generally only shown where they intersect the red trails.

Do I need other Maps?

While it's possible to hike the trails using the maps in this book, why not take along a 1:50000 recreation map by Gem Trek? They are available at most outdoor stores, bookstores and gas stations in the region. The four that cover the trails in this book are:

Canmore and Kananaskis Village
(Trails #1-12, 18, 34-35)
Kananaskis Lakes (#13-17, 19-21)
Highwood and Cataract Creek (#22-25)
Bragg Creek and Elbow Falls (#26-35).

What to wear for the trails

Be prepared for fast weather changes and pack raingear. For walks and scrambles above treeline take a wind jacket, long pants and extra warm clothing. During the summer a sun hat, sun cream and mosquito repellent are must-takes. Light hiking boots suffice for all the trails in this book.

Doing More

If you have enjoyed the trails in this book why not hike more trails in Kananaskis Country? *Canmore & Kananaskis Country: Short Walks for Inquiring Minds* covers all the interpretive trails and other short walks suitable for the less active or for families with young children.

Kananaskis Country Trail Guide volumes 1 and 2 cover all of K Country plus the Bow Valley, The Ghost and Elk Lakes Provincial Park. They are comprehensive, and describe all designated and undesignated trails, long-distance trails, backpacks, easy scrambles and ridgewalks.

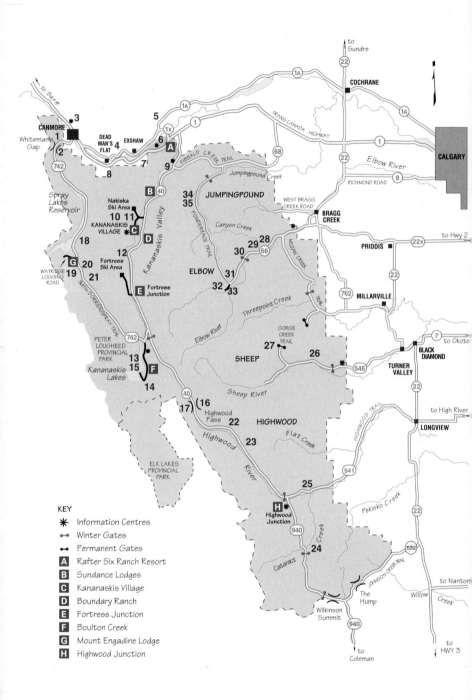

KEY

✳	Information Centres
●━●	Winter Gates
●━	Permanent Gates
A	Rafter Six Ranch Resort
B	Sundance Lodges
C	Kananaskis Village
D	Boundary Ranch
E	Fortress Junction
F	Boulton Creek
G	Mount Engadine Lodge
H	Highwood Junction

The Trails

1 *Grassi Lakes*

Distance 3.8 km return
Height gain 244 m
High Point 1670 m
Easy
Late spring, summer, fall

Two exquisite blue lakes, views of mountains and waterfalls, interpretive signs and plentiful benches make this everybody's favourite short day hike.

Start: Canmore. Follow Spray Lakes Road (Hwy. 762) past the Canmore Nordic Centre. At the next road junction turn left onto a road signed "Spray Residences." Turn first right into the trailhead parking lot.

Difficulty: A good, well-marked trail to the lakes with one short moderately steep section with steps.

1. From the biffy a short trail leads to the TransAlta access road (alias Upper Grassi Lakes trail). Turn right. Shortly turn left off the road onto Grassi's trail.

2. The trail traverses pine hillside, all the time gradually climbing. Cross a number of springs just before reaching a viewpoint with interpretive signs. Look down on Rundle Canal and across to Ha Ling Peak.

3. The trail turns right and zigs uphill. To your left is a view of the waterfall below Lower Grassi Lake. Higher up the trail surmounts a weeping wall by resorting to stone steps safeguarded by a wooden railing. At the top is a bench. Another zig leads into a long traverse to the left. At its end you bridge the creek from the lower lake and join the TransAlta access road at a T-junction.

View of the waterfall from 3.

4. Turn right on the road. Just before re-crossing the creek, turn left onto the trail continued.

5. The trail follows the shoreline of the lower lake to a junction. Keep left and in a few minutes arrive at the upper lake. The trail follows the shoreline to the far end where the good trail ends.

At 2 carnivorous Butterworts grow around the springs in profusion.

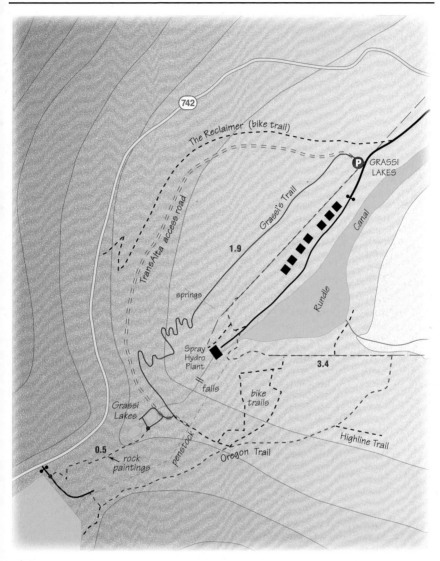

6. Return to the previous junction between the lakes. Turn left.

7. The trail bridges the creek between the two lakes. On your right is the plaque honouring Lawrence Grassi who built the original trail in the 1920s. At a T-junction turn right (bench to left) and arrive back on the TransAlta access road.

8. To return, turn right, cross the creek, then turn next left onto Grassi's trail.

9. Alternately, on reaching the TransAlta access road you can turn left and follow it all the way out to the parking lot. It's a boring walk in the trees, the only point of interest being the ruins of a log cabin at the half-way point.

The Steps at 3.

Lower Grassi Lake, looking toward EEOR (the East End of Rundle).

Upper Grassi Lake from the northwest shore.

Above: Pictograph at O2 believed painted over 1000 years ago by ancestors of the Kootenai, likely as part of a vision quest.

Right: View from the scree chute at O1 of climbers on the Golf Course, so named because of the abundance of holes in the rock.

Going farther to the Dam

Distance add on 0.9 km return
Height gain add on 90 m

A very much rougher trail up through the canyon to Whitemans Dam with steps fashioned out of rock and wood. Grades are occasionally steep and the footing loose on scree and boulders.

1. From the far end of upper Grassi Lake a steep climber's trail ascends the left side of the scree chute into the canyon above.

2. After the trail levels, look for the large pictograph boulder on the right. The paintings of a man and a caribou are roped off and interpretive-signed.

3. Pick your way over rocks where you might spot a pika.

4. Suddenly the canyon is blocked by the earth wall of the dam. Climb steps alongside the right-hand crag, then follow the winding trail up scree to the top of the dam. Ahead is Whitemans Pond (reservoir).

The steps up from the canyon at O4 onto the face of Whitemans Dam.

Left: Oregon trail at O4. This was the route taken by early nineteenth century travellers journeying between the prairies and Oregon. From the Canmore area it climbed to Whitemans Pass, followed the Spray River a way, then crossed over White Man Pass into B.C.

Below: In late Spring Yellow Sparrows Egg orchids grow in profusion under the powerlines.

Optional descent via Oregon Trail and the powerline

Distance 3.4 km to trailhead

From the dam, Oregon trail enables you to make a 5.8 km loop back to the parking lot. The route is occasionally marked and has moderate downhill grades easing off to flat. Near the end is a short uphill climb to a powerline.

1. Turn left and walk along the dam. To right is Whitemans Pond and a view through the gap of the Goat Range. The road curves left past the penstock and ends.

2. Turn right and on a short stretch of trail climb uphill into forest. At the T-junction with historic Oregon Trail turn left. (Trail to right heads for the reservoir and disappears underwater.)

3. The trail descends under the north face of Ha Ling Peak to a T-junction. Go straight. (Trail to left leads to the end of the TransAlta access road.)

4. Continue descending past the junction with Highline Trail. The grade moderates lower down where you cross runnels of scree and flattens out before reaching the powerline (signpost). Turn left.

5. Follow the powerline access road, ultimately winding down a hill to cross the bridge over Rundle Canal. To your left is Spray Hydro Plant, to your right the controversial wildlife bridge. Reach the hydro plant access road.

6. There is the option of turning right and simply walking along the road to the parking lot. I prefer to cross the road onto a trail.

7. Shortly the trail joins another powerline access road. Turn left and climb straight up a steep hill to the powerline right-of-way. Turn right and follow it out to the parking lot.

2 *Ha Ling Peak*

Distance 5.6 km return
Height gain 732 m
High point 2408 m
Strenuous
Late spring, summer, fall

Start: Hwy. 742 (Smith-Dorrien—Spray Trail) at Whiteman's Gap. Park in the Goat Creek parking lot just south of Whiteman's Pond.

Difficulty: Initially a good trail with switchbacks up a steep forested slope. Higher up the trail is on scree. The final ascent is on shale and rubble and though hands are not needed, a little routefinding may be required.

A muscle-aching grind up the west slope of Ha Ling Peak, the prominent mountain overlooking Canmore and a fabulous viewpoint. From the saddle between the mountain and Miners Peak, both peaks are accessible.

Ha Ling Peak from Whitemans Pond. The route goes up the easy west face on the right skyline.

1. Cross the highway, walk up a road to the canal and cross it via the bridge. The Ha Ling/Miners Peak Trail starts behind the hut at a cairn.

2. Initially the trail meanders through a beautiful moss forest.

3. At the foot of the steep slope and by the side of a gully the trail makes a few preliminary zigs, then makes a long zig to the left. On the long zig back right you cross "the slab" and then "the rib." This brings you back to the gully. Again zig left, then back right to a cairn. From here the trail corkscrews straight up to treeline. Turn right into "Leon's Traverse" where the trail makes a long rising traverse below the screes of Ha Ling Peak. At last trees, it corkscrews uphill a bit, then sweeps left to the saddle between Ha Ling on the left and Miners Peak on the right.

4. Keep left and pick your way up the rocky southeast ridge to the top. There's no one route; just innumerable trails etched in scree and shale winding about easy-angled slabs. The cairn is perched right on the edge of the eastern abyss and offers a birds-eye view of Canmore and the Bow Valley.

The forest trail at 3. Photo David Wasserman.

The slab traverse at 3. This photo was taken before the latest improvement which did away with the handrail.

Today's trail was built by the Trailminders of Canmore and is a far cry from the exceedingly steep eroded trail up by the side of the gully.

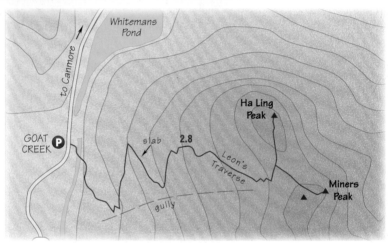

On Leon's Traverse at 3. In the background are unnamed humps located on the ridge between Ha Ling and Mt. Lawrence Grassi.

The whole range is known as Ehagay Nakoda. It's a Stoney name meaning "the last Nakoda [Stoney]" who was transformed into a mountain in order to "remain on this Earth long after all human beings cease to inhabit it."

Above: The upper part of Ha Ling Peak, showing the saddle, the trail at 4 and the eastern precipice overlooking Canmore.

In 1896, Ha Ling, a Chinese cook working in Canmore, was bet 50 dollars he couldn't climb up and down within 10 hours. He made it in a 5 hour round trip—a remarkable time that can hardly be bettered today. Not surprisingly no one believed him, so the next day he led a group of doubters to the top where his flag was seen *"proudly flapping in the breeze."* *"As the peak has no name let it hence forth be called Ha Ling Peak in honour of his daring intrepidity"* it was proclaimed. For many generations, though, it was called *"Chinaman's Peak."* Then during the Great Canmore Influx of the 1990s the name officially changed to Ha Ling. To this day there are pockets of resistance to the new name by long-time locals.

Centre: The summit on the edge. In this photo the hikers are looking south to Pigeon Mountain.

Bottom: Heading back down from the summit there is a new view of Goat Creek valley with the tip of Goat Pond just showing.

Option Miners Peak

Height gain 50 m from col

An easier option to Ha Ling that can also be climbed on the same trip.

1. At the saddle head up right along the slowly rising ridgeline. When it flattens turn left and walk out on a slightly exposed promontory (cliffs on both sides) to the summit of Miners Peak.

Below top: View from the saddle showing the easy ridge leading past the three humps to Mt. Lawrence Grassi, which is seen poking up in the background. Miners Peak is the promontory at left. Though it is scarcely a peak from this direction, from Canmore it appears quite prominent.

Below bottom: Miners Peak (left) from the ridge. From this angle it shows the narrow nature of the promontory.

3 *Teahouse Ridge*

Distance 8 km return
Height gain 853 m
High point 2225 m
Strenuous
Late spring, summer, fall

Start: Canmore. Drive Elk Run Boulevard to a parking lot on the left (west) side of the bridge over Cougar Creek.

Difficulty: A good to fair marked trail with moderately steep grades throughout. Cairns and branches or rocks laid across old trails keep you on the right track. Expect some shale, scree and rocks underfoot. Being southwest facing, the slope bakes on hot summer days, so carry up lots of water.

1. From the parking lot follow the paved Cougar Creek trail along the northwest bank of Cougar Creek. After the trail reverts to normal, keep straight at two T-junctions. (Trails to left are Montane Traverse and the old trail up Lady MacDonald.) Turn left at the third T-junction with signpost. (Ahead is Cougar Creek trail.)

2. The Lady MacDonald Trail, improved in recent years by Trailminders, takes a rising diagonal line up the grassy bank into the trees, the main trail always obvious. Old trails have branches laid across them.

3. Above these "junctions" the trail winds up the easy-angled portion of Teahouse Ridge. Then after a meadow viewpoint (short detour to left), it gets steep and twisty, this section ending at a small rock step where the trail goes more easily left to a junction of old and new trails.

4. Zig right onto the east face, then make a long zig back left, en route passing a bench and crossing the old route at the scree slope. A zig back right meets the old route again and follows it up a short way before taking off left.

The reward for a trudge up Teahouse Ridge on Lady MacDonald is a fabulous view of the Bow Valley.

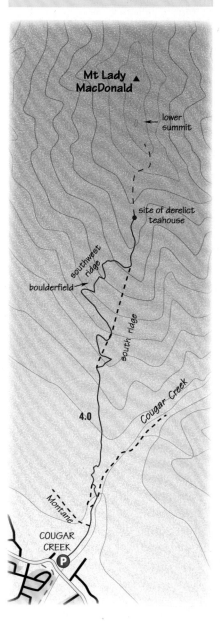

Leaving the parking lot on the paved Cougar Creek trail. Above rises Mt. Lady MacDonald. The teahouse site is located on the flattening at treeline.

The trail zigs across scree slopes at 4. Already there is a fine view looking out across the Bow Valley to Mt. Rundle.

Left: The trail at 7, climbing alongside the rockband on the east side of the south ridge.

Opposite: The helipad at the end of the main trail. Above rises Lady MacDonald, the main summit at left. Carrying on is a much rougher trail up the scree to the summit ridge.

5. This time the trail sweeps nearly all the way across the southwest face beneath a large meadow. Slabs force the trail to turn right into a small boulderfield. Follow cairns and flagging up the left edge of the boulders and into a steep twisting climb ending on the open southwest ridge.

6. Plod up the ridge on shale and clamber over a few rocks. Not too far below the apex of the southwest face the trail turns right and traverses to the south ridge. Meet up with the old route at flagging and turn left.

Approaching the unfinished teahouse.

7. After a short climb you cross a perpendicular rock band onto the more verdant east side of the ridge which is followed up to a levelling. The half-built derelict teahouse is located a little higher up the ridge at treeline. The first floor roof and the helipad make good places for a tick-free sit down. Down to your right is the gazebo. Above you the ridge rises to the summit ridge of Lady MacDonald. Below is a panoramic view of the Bow Valley.

The gazebo in its heyday.

Going farther to the summit ridge of Lady Macdonald

Distance return add 0.6 km
Extra height gain 274 m
High point 2499 m

A more difficult option for hikers who can handle scree and rubble on poor trails. The grade is moderately steep.

1. The trail continues up the next rise in the ridge to a levelling with rusted takeoff ramp for paragliders.

2. Above rises a wall of rubble and a few small slabs. Initially follow the trail uphill. Then, rather than be lured by trails heading straight up, walkers should follow the yellow scree trail that heads diagonally right, passing **below** a perpendicular slab before turning uphill. Here I recommend treading the firmer scree to one side of the trail and reserving the "trail" for a fun fast descent.

3. Arrive on the summit ridge of Lady MacDonald and head up left to a cairn. Unless you can handle difficult exposed scrambling go no farther. The ridge narrows with slabs on one side and a vertical drop on the other.

Left: The wall of rubble from the end of O1. In this fore-shortened view the perpendicular rockband can be seen not far below the skyline, sloping from left to right. The trail you want passes below it before heading uphill. At far left is the main summit of the mountain.

Below: The cairn marks the end of the road for most people.

4 Grotto Canyon

Distance 4.2 km return to forks,
10.8 km return to head of valley
Height gain 480 m to head of valley
Fairly easy
Early spring, summer, fall

Start: Hwy. 1A (Bow Valley Trail) at Grotto Pond day-use area.

Difficulty: A good well marked trail initially. Then a poor trail following a stoney creekbed with many minor creek crossings on rocks. In spring run-off or after rain the creek may be impassable.

1. From the trailhead follow the stoney powerline right-of-way access road. Cross the access road to Enviro Enterprises quarry and continue on the right-of-way. Ahead is the noisy Baymag Plant II.

2. Level with the plant, turn right onto a signed trail that heads across an alluvial flat. Keep right at a junction with the climber's access trail.

3. On the bank of Grotto Creek, the trail turns upstream, following the stoney creek bed into the canyon. Cross to and fro between vertical cliffs. Watch for rock paintings, low down and barely discernible, on a smooth slab to the left.

4. Arrive at the forks below a high cliff. To right, most of the water in the creek tumbles over a low cliff.

5. Go left. This is where the cliffs on either side attain their greatest height.

6. The valley floor widens and the walls on either side fall back a little. Note a capped hoodoo on the right bank and then the huge block of eroded tillite on the left.

7. Wander up the valley between Grotto Mountain and Gap Peak as far as you have time for. The trail continues on one bank or the other for another 2.5 km. En route you pass numerous climber's crags.

Walk through a spectacular canyon known for its pictographs. You're sure to be entertained by rock climbers.

At 2, crossing the flat en route to the canyon. In the background rises the south end of Grotto Mountain.

Climbers on Short and Curly on Three Tier Buttress. Photo John Martin.

Above: Grotto Falls at the forks at 4.

Top left: The narrows at 5.

Bottom left: The pictograph slab at 3.

Bottom right: Computer enhanced image of a figure by James Henderson. It was only a few years ago that archeologist Marty Magne theorized the petrographs were painted as far back as 1,300 years ago by the Hopi of Arizona. On the other hand, a Stoney historian believes they were painted by Stoneys who journeyed south and based the images on what they saw. Look for a flute player, a moose kill and a line of human figures all painted in the Hopi style.

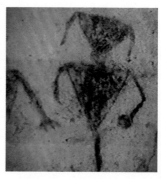

Eroded tillite higher up the valley at 6.

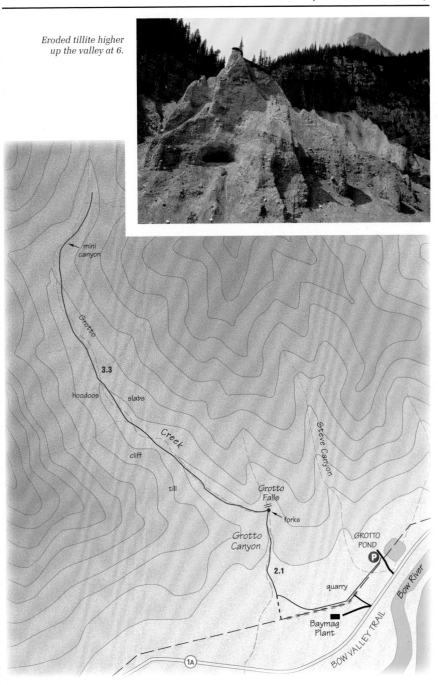

mini canyon

Grotto

3.3

hoodoos   slabs

Creek

cliff

till

Steve Canyon

Grotto Falls

forks

Grotto Canyon

2.1

quarry

GROTTO POND

P

Bow River

Baymag Plant

BOW VALLEY TRAIL

1A

5 Raven's End

Distance 7 km return
Height gain 520 m
High point 1890 m
Moderate
Often year round

Start: Hwy. 1A (Bow Valley Trail). 2.1 km east of 1X Highway turn left (north) onto the quarry road. Keep straight, then turn left into a parking lot.

Difficulty: A good trail, occasionally marked, with a few steep sections. These hills are very slippery when wet. Minor route-finding.

Close to the parking lot is Beaver Dam Lake. Its grassy bank makes a fine place for relaxation after the hike.

1. Starting from the far end of the parking lot at the kiosk, your trail runs parallel to the quarry road. It crosses a grassy track and then the quarry road itself to the climber's registration box.

2. From here the trail undulates through flowery aspen forest, crosses a cutline, then a track in a dip. Join another track briefly, then leave it and climb very steeply to the top of a sandstone escarpment by way of a break.

3. At the top is a 4-way junction with sign. (Straight on is the climber's access trail to

A moderately steep climb to the east ridge of Yamnuska known as Raven's End

Yamnuska.) Turn right on a narrower trail. Shortly it intersects the old track from the quarry. Turn right.

4. A flat section through woods ends at a creek crossing that is usually dry. This signals the start of the climb to the east ridge, which is not as bad as it looks. You will not be flogging up the steep stoney track.

5. Your trail continues ahead, then zigs back left, crossing the stoney track toward the creek. Keep left on the trail at junctions with the track.

6. Halfway up, trail and track merge and you traverse right onto a grassy bench, the first of many good viewpoints. A short climb leads onto another bench. Almost at once the trail divides. Keep right. (To left is a steep shortcut.)

7. Follow the traverse to the next junction marked by a cairn. Turn left. (The trail continuing along the bench is a horse trail that leads to the boundary fence with the Stoney Reserve and ultimately to the South Ghost valley.)

8. The gentler trail soon reaches the treed east ridge and follows it along. Keep straight where the shortcut comes in from the left. A short steep uphill precedes a T-junction with cairn. Turn left. (Straight on is the trail into CMC Valley.)

9. The trail, heading straight for Yamnuska, winds about in the pines and for walkers ends where it abuts against the rock of this great cliff. You have reached Raven's End. Here your own trail downgrades to an exposed scramble up the rock ridge to the summit. To left a climber's descent route plummets down the hillside.

10. Return the same way

Yamnuska from the trail between 2 and 3. The name is derived from the Stoney name meaning "Wall of Stone." It is the birthplace of modern rock climbing in the Canadian Rockies.

Between 2 and 3, trees tied with cloth signify a Stoney offering of prayers to the creator.

Yamnuska from the lower traverse at 6. Where the ridge and cliff meet is Raven's End.

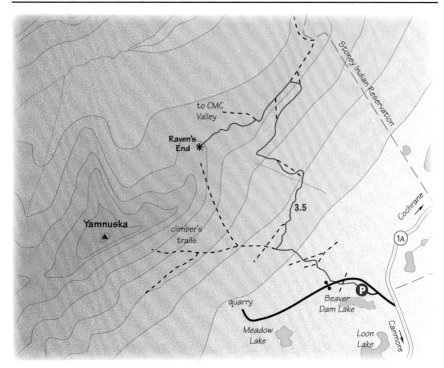

to CMC Valley

Raven's End

Yamnuska

climber's trails

3.5

Stoney Indian Reservation

Cochrane

1A

quarry

Meadow Lake

Beaver Dam Lake

P

Loon Lake

Canmore

Looking back from the upper traverse at 7 toward Yamnuska and Raven's End.

From 7 a late fall view over the Bow Valley, showing the numerous ponds glittering against the low sunlight. The mountain in the centre foreground is Yates Mountain, climbed by route #9.

The trail junction on the east ridge at 8. Looking north across CMC Valley is Mt. Wendell, another climber's hot spot.

Ben Gadd at Raven's End. The meeting of the east ridge with the great cliff is immortalized in Gadd's book of the same title. This is a good place to spot the "wildies" as opposed to the "townies" as Ben calls the ravens. Photo Chic Scott.

6 Bow Valley Provincial Park Loop

Distance 8.7 km loop
Height gain 156 m
Easy
Often year round

Start: The Trans-Canada Hwy. (Hwy. 1) at the Seebe interchange. Turn off onto Hwy. 1X. Turn first left onto the park road. Drive past the visitor centre to Middle Lake parking lot. You can also pick up the trail from Bow Valley campground, Whitefish day-use area, Many Springs parking lot and Elk Flats day-use area. **Note:** The park roads are closed beyond Middle Lake from mid-October to mid-May.

Difficulty: Easy, well-marked trails with a few short hills.

Moraine Trail on the crest of a moraine at 4. Looking toward Goat Mountain.

Though it appears flat, Bow Valley Provincial Park is really quite bumpy. Glacial advances and retreats have left behind a fascinating topography of moraines, eskers, kames, crevasse fillings, and kettles sometimes filled with water.

An amalgamation of six interpretive trails wanders through a varied landscape of moraines, riversides and lakeshores in a kaleidoscope of pine forest and dry meadows. Flowers are spectacular around late June-early July. Picnic tables, benches and biffies all the way around.

Anti-clockwise

1. From the parking lot head down Moraine Trail to Middle Lake. At the T-junction on the east shore turn right.

2. Follow reed-fringed Moraine Trail along the east and north shores of the lake to the park road. En route is a bench and interpretive sign.

3. Cross the road. The trail continues on the other side to a T-junction with Elk Flats trail. Keep straight on Moraine Trail.

4. The trail winds onto the top of an open moraine (interpretive signs) and follows

the crest, ultimately dropping off the end into trees. Cross a powerline right-of-way and descend to Bow Valley campground. You pass the amphitheatre on your right and by keeping left arrive on the main campground access road.

5. A signed trail crosses the main campground access road and then B Loop. Continue to C Loop. An unsigned trail carries on to a T-junction with Bow River Trail on the banks of the Bow River. Turn left.

6. The Bow River Trail follows the river bank within reach of campsites in C loop. There's a gap, then it runs alongside E loop. Keep straight at the end of E loop and arrive on the fringe of Whitefish day-use area parking lot in a meadow. If making for the picnic tables and biffy, keep straight and cross the parking lot. Otherwise, turn left onto Whitefish Trail. Keep straight. (Trail coming in from the right is the official start to the trail from the parking lot.)

Western wood lilies in late June. Other flowers to look for include Northern blue columbines, various orchids, and on calcareous flats the beautiful Prairie gentians and oddly shaped Elephantheads.

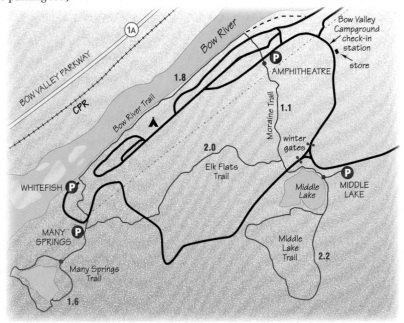

29

7. Whitefish Trail climbs up the bank and crosses a powerline right-of-way, then the park road. At a T-junction turn right into Many Springs parking lot with its interesting interpretive sign.

8. Set off down Many Spring Trail, a wide gravel track at this point. At a junction turn right onto a narrower trail, going counter-clockwise around the basin loop.

9. Descend slightly and on reaching a powerline right-of-way turn left.

10. Follow the right-of-way to Many Springs Lake at a beaver dam. Here the trail heads right and crosses the outlet on a bridge overlooking a channel of the Bow River.

11. The trail continues ahead then turns left. Cross under the powerlines and descend once again to the lakeshore. Initially follow boardwalk, then move inland onto drier ground in the forest where the beavers have been busy lopping trees. Reach the far end viewing platform that once overlooked springs bubbling out of the ground but which now looks over the lake toward Yamnuska. From here the trail climbs out of the basin and reverts to wide gravel track. Keep straight and arrive back at the parking lot.

12. Turn right, then at the T-junction keep straight on Elk Flats Trail that climbs to the park road.

13. Cross the road opposite Elk Flats day-use area parking lot. A little way in is a T-junction. Keep straight. (Trail to left leads to Elk Flats group camp and day-use area.)

14. The trail meanders from one stoney meadow to another, the terrain becoming hillier as you approach the T-junction with Moraine Trail.

15. Turn right on Moraine Trail. Cross the park road and follow the trail along the north and east shores of Middle Lake to a junction.

16. Either turn left and return to Middle Lake parking lot (deduct 2.2 km) or continue ahead on Middle Lake Trail.

17. At the next junction keep left, walking clockwise around the loop that is mostly forested with a few small meadows. The final leg runs along the scenic south shore (two viewing benches) back to the T-junction. Turn left.

18. At the junction on the east shore turn right and return to Middle Lake parking lot.

Interpretive sign at Whitefish Day-use Area. In the background is the Bow River and Yamnuska.

Many Springs Trail at the viewpoint at 11. This picture shows the springs bubbling up from out of the ground, and was taken before the beavers dammed the outlet and made the basin into a lake. In the distance is Yamnuska.

Elk Flats Trail at 14 between Elk Flats parking lot and Moraine Trail junction. Stony meadows are covered in juniper and kinnikinnick.

Reed-fringed Middle Lake from the parking lot trail at 1 and 18. Looking west toward the Three Sisters above Canmore. To right is Exshaw Mountain.

7 *Heart Mountain Circuit*

Distance 9.7 km return
Height gain 930 m
High point 2149 m
Strenuous
Late spring, summer, fall

Perhaps K Country's most popular ridgewalk, the Heart Mountain circuit takes in several tops. Do the whole loop or just climb to Heart Mountain and back.

Start: Trans-Canada Hwy. (Hwy. 1). At Lac des Arcs interchange follow signs to Heart Creek parking lot.

Difficulty: You start and finish on good well-marked trails. In between a poor to fair trail follows the ridgeline around. On the ascent to Heart Mountain the trail is marked with red markers and arrows. While there is no exposure anywhere on this route, the ascent and descent ridges are steep and route-finding is necessary on scree and rock. Expect easy scrambling and one unavoidable moderate pitch up a rockband. Creeks are bridged.

1. From the parking lot head east on Heart Creek Trail that climbs around a ridge before descending to Heart Creek valley. Bridge the creek to a 5-way junction on the east bank.

2. Heart Mountain trail (third from the left) is marked by a yellow warning sign.

3. The trail follows the northwest ridge of Heart Mountain up an initial step.

After an easing the ridge steepens, with numerous trails winding about scree and broken rock. In all the mess search out the zigging trail. Arriving at the base of a crag, either tackle it direct or follow a trail to the left into trees. Both routes join below another steepening with easy scrambling up cracks. The terrain eases off again and you come to the crux below the "heart."

4. Above is the rockband. Red metal tags mark the spot where you scramble up 4 m of vertical rock to a small cairn.

5. The upper ridge, easy at first, steepens into slabs. Follow the trail into the yellow gully to the left of the slabs, and where the gully steepens, escape right (red metal tag) to a small tree on the gully's right-hand edge. Above all difficulties, walk up to the first top which is Heart Mountain.

To right is Heart Mountain, showing the ascent ridge rising from the bottom right-hand corner. Going left is the tip of Grant MacEwan Peak, then tops #3 and #4. The descent ridge leaves top #4 and descends to the bottom left-hand corner.

The upper half of the ascent ridge rising to Heart Mountain. The crux occurs two-thirds up the ridge above the treed ledge.

The crux at 4 is 4 m of moderate scrambling and not as easy as it looks. It starts with a slight overhang and a high step up left.

The head of the yellow gully where you traverse right to the gully edge at 5. Photo Cal Damen, courtesy Rob Laird.

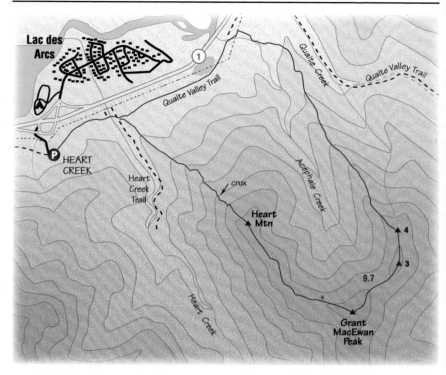

6. The trail continues over minor humps then climbs a narrowing stoney ramp with slabs on both sides to the highest top of the day. This is Grant McEwan Peak, a broad summit where three ridges meet.

7. Heading northeast, the trail descends a broad grass ridge dotted with trees to a col, then regaining nearly all the height lost, zigs up scree to top #3.

8. Traverse north along a narrower ridge to top #4 at the head of the descent ridge.

9. The trail descends another northwest ridge. Initially it makes a few lazy turns in scree, then heads down a scree ramp to the right of the rocky ridge crest. Lower down the ridge broadens, long flat areas in meadows or in trees alternating with scree and slabby scramble steps.

10. Enter pine forest. The slabby steps continue for a while. Then comes a long steep rooty downclimb after which the angle moderates and the trail improves.

11. Low down above Acephale Creek keep right. (First trail to left leads to Acephale Waterfall.) Other trails lead to the creek for water!

12. Reach a powerline. Turn left. Before reaching the creek the trail turns right, crosses the creek, which is usually dry at this point, and intersects the much larger Quaite Valley Trail west of the bridge.

13. Turn left on Quaite Valley Trail. It crosses under the powerline, passes a small pond alongside the Trans-Canada Highway and heads for the 5-way junction on the east bank of Heart Creek. The going is quite pleasant in aspen forest.

14. Go straight, cross the bridge over Heart Creek and climb the hill back to the parking lot.

The summit of Grant MacEwan Peak, named in 2006 after Alberta's lieutenant governor, prolific writer and man of the people. Photo Tony Daffern.

Above: View from near the summit of Grant MacEwan Peak of the undulating ridge connecting to Heart Mountain at 6.

Descending Grant MacEwan Peak at 7, you get this view of top #3 (centre) and top #4 (left). The descent ridge follows the ridge at left.

Looking back from top #3 at the gentle slopes of Grant MacEwan Peak.

Below: Looking back along the ridge from top #4 to top #3. To left is Barrier Lake.

Looking up at the descent ridge to top #4.

8 Wind Ridge

Distance 13.8 km return
Height gain 740 m
High point 2164 m
Moderately strenuous
Late spring, summer, fall
Trail is open June 16 to Nov. 30

Start: Trans-Canada Highway (Hwy. 1). At Dead Man's Flat interchange follow signs to Banff Gate Mountain Resort. At the final bend, turn right into Pigeon Mountain trailhead.

Difficulty: Ranges from exploration roads to a well-used trail. Moderately steep sections near the end include one pitch of easy scrambling. For hikers who don't wish to scramble, Wind Point is the easier option.

A forest walk up Wind Valley followed by an entertaining climb up a grassy ridge to the summit of Wind Ridge.

1. From the far end of the parking lot at the kiosk head out on a dirt track that is an exploration road.

2. Cross the powerline. (To left is Skogan Pass Trail.)

3. Wind downhill and cross a bridge over Pigeon Creek. On the far bank turn right at a T-junction with another exploration road. (To left is the northern part of the Centennial Ridge Trail over Mt. Allan.)

4. Shortly cross the bridge over West Wind Creek. At the next junction turn left.

5. The road heads up Wind Valley, winding through spruce forest alongside West Wind Creek. To right and left are a number of overgrown side roads.

6. Ultimately the road turns sharp right and climbs through Douglas fir forest to a T-junction. Turn left.

7. Your new road leads out onto the meadows of Wind Ridge's southeast face.

8. The road degenerates to trail that curves up right to gain the east ridge below a fringe of trees. (Wind Point to right.)

9. The main trail heads left below the ridge line. Very shortly keep left at a split. On gaining the ridge proper, ascend rather more steeply, weaving between small crags to the base of a rock band.

10. Climb up to a ledge, either directly or from the left and traverse right along it until you can escape up left.

11. The trail continues in much the same way as before to the summit ridge. All that remains is an easy stroll to the cairn and geodetic survey marker. Look across Stewart Creek to the Three Sisters.

Wind Ridge, showing the trail curving up grass to the low point on the ridge. To right is Wind Point. The main trail follows the ridgeline to the summit at far left.

Easier option to Wind Point

Distance 11.2 km return from trailhead
Height gain 410 m from trailhead

An option for hikers who don't want to scramble. The going is easy on a fair trail.

1. From where you first gain the ridge crest at 8 head right, following a less distinct trail in grass at the edge of the trees. It meanders above steep grassy slopes to a viewpoint with survey marker marking the abrupt end of the east ridge.

2. The view is mainly to the south and east. Trees obscure the view northwards.

*Douglas fir along the road
between 6 and 7.*

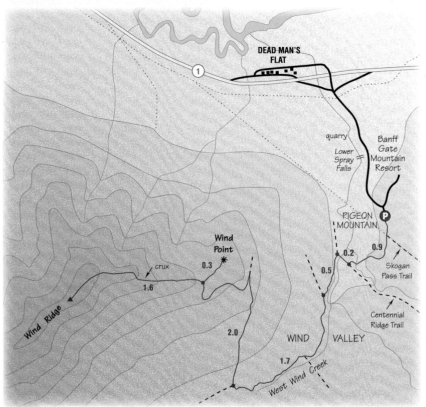

Windtower from the traverse at 7.

On the east ridge at 9, heading for the rockband.

At 10. Reaching the ledge at the crux.

The view from 11. The ridge above the rockband is easy, the trail winding around a few small crags. The summit is at far left.

On the summit. In the background is West Wind Pass at left, Rimwall at centre and The Orphan at right. If you have time you can continue the ridgewalk along the ridge to the start of the scree.

9 *Barrier Lake Lookout*

Distance 10.6 km return
Height gain 616 m
High point 1996 m
Moderate
Late spring, summer, fall

Start: Hwy. 40 (Kananaskis Trail) at Barrier Dam day-use area.

Difficulty: Good well-marked trail with moderate grades apart from one short steep rocky section onto McConnell Ridge. From here the unmarked trail to the lookout is generally good. The steep section has loose footing.

1. Head out on the gravel track beyond the gate. Keep left and cross the dam. (To right is the access road to Barrier Substation.)

2. At the far end cross under a powerline, then in a reclaimed meadow follow either the track or a trail to its right up a hill. At the top cross a powerline right-of-way with signpost. (To left is Jewell Pass trail.)

3. The track climbs to a T-junction with another track (Stoney Trail). Turn right, then straightaway left on what used to be the Pigeon Lookout fire road. It is signposted Prairie View Trail.

4. Closeted in trees, the fire road winds uphill in easy zigs, at the end of the 11th and final zig turning left onto a northeast ridge. (At this bend the unsigned Lookout trail from Camp Chief Hector comes in from the right.)

Barrier Lake Lookout atop Yates Mountain is an irresistible objective promising a fabulous view.

5. The fire road continues uphill, then levels at the site of Pigeon Lookout. To the left meadows slope down toward Barrier Lake and are a popular rest stop.

6. The road ends not too much farther on. A trail carries on, zigging left, then right and up a rocky step to a T-junction on McConnell Ridge. To your right is a TransAlta repeater station. Step out left to a viewpoint above a cliff.

7. At the T-junction turn right. Ahead rises the highest point of McConnell Ridge which is known as Yates Mountain. The trail is a little nebulous at first, but soon becomes clear as it starts the climb up the forested ridge. The going is moderately steep for two thirds of the way, then slackens right off. At a split go either way—left is a scree trail, right is a walk along the edge of a cliff. After they join, one final uphill burst gains you the summit. It's a big open area of grass and rocks almost entirely occupied by the lookout, the helipad, two masts, and assorted sheds and instruments.

8. Return the same way. At the T-junction near the repeater station you can decide if you want to do the loop.

Yates Mountain. The route more or less follows the left skyline to the summit.

Looking up at McConnell Ridge from the fire road near the Pigeon Lookout site between 5 and 6. To right is Yates Mountain.

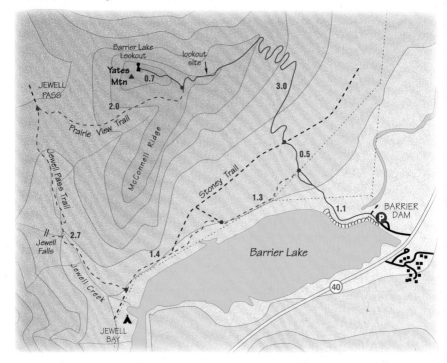

The viewpoint on McConnell Ridge at 6. The peak above Barrier Lake is Mt. Baldy.

The summit picture on Canada Day. Looking northwest down the Bow Valley toward Canmore. In the left middle ground is Grant MacEwan Peak and tops #3 and #4 of the Heart Mountain Circuit.

Barrier Lake Lookout atop Yates Mountain.

Optional return via Jewell Pass

13.1 km circuit
Add 1.4 km and 125 m height gain if you
include the lookout in the outing.

A loop can be made by returning via Jewell
Pass Trail. This predominantly forest trail is
well marked and while the grade is easy
overall, there are a few short steep steps.

1. At the T-junction on McConnell Ridge
turn left if missing out the climb to Barrier
Lake Lookout, or continue straight if you
have just come down from the lookout.

2. Prairie View Trail descends the ridge
line above a line of crags. Keep an eye out
for marmots sunning themselves on the
rocks. At a col it turns right, heading down
and back right into dense Lodgepole pine
forest about Jewell Pass. At a T-junction
with signpost turn left. (To right is Quaite
Valley Trail.)

3. Initially Jewell Pass Trail descends very
gradually into Jewell Creek valley. En
route you jump the tiny north fork. A very
much steeper zigzag descent brings you to
the forks. Bridge the main west creek just
below the confluence. Straightaway a side
trail to right leads to tiny Jewell Falls.

4. Continue down the main trail, first on
the right bank of Jewell Creek, then on
the left bank for a much longer steeper
stretch. To get around the upcoming bend
the trail climbs to a terrace that is followed
all around the base of McConnell Ridge.
Descend under a powerline to intersect
Stoney Trail (cutline access road) at a T-
junction. (To right, a mere 200 m away, is
Jewell Bay backcountry campground with
seats and picnic tables.)

5. Turn left. Follow the cutline access road
to an intersection with the powerline.
Turn right onto a trail with hiking sign.

6. Head through meadow above Barrier Lake. Shortly the main trail heads
slightly downhill to the left. At the following split keep left on the trail that
undulates around a bay and joins with
a track. Again go left. (The track to right
ends in the water.) In a few metres reach
a T-junction with a powerline access road
at a trail sign. Go straight. (Left leads back
to Stoney Trail.)

7. The undulating powerline access road
delivers you back to your outgoing track
at the signpost. Turn right and return the
same way you came up.

Jewell Pass signpost at the end of O2. To left is Prairie View Trail, to right Jewell Pass Trail. The pass is entirely enclosed in trees. But by following the Quaite Creek Trail for a short distance to a 4-way junction you get a view of top #4 of the Heart Mountain Horseshoe.

Jewell Falls on the main west fork of Jewell Creek is easily reached by a trail along the left bank. It is best after rain. By mid summer it dries to a trickle.

The trail alongside Jewell Creek at 4, just before it starts to climb around the bend.

10 *Centennial Ridge of Mount Allan*

Distance 14.4 km return
Height gain 1359 m
High point 2819 m
Strenuous
Summer after June 21, early fall

Start: Kananaskis Trail (Hwy. 40). Turn west onto the road to Nakiska Ski Area (Mt. Allan Drive). Turn first left onto Centennial Drive, then next right onto Ribbon Creek Road. Drive to the far end parking lot (picnic shelter, picnic tables, biffy).

Difficulty: A good trail on steep slopes with switchbacks. Expect both grass and scree, and two pitches of easy scrambling. Well-marked with signposts, cairns and red paint splodges on rocks.

The Centennial Ridge Trail is the highest trail ever built in the Canadian Rockies—a suitably impressive route to the summit of Mt. Allan. The trail traverses the mountain to Pigeon Mountain trailhead, but most people just go up and down from Ribbon Creek.

1. Starting from the near right-hand corner of the parking lot, follow Hidden Trail as it curves up left and into a straight. (Do NOT cross the tiny creek onto the original Marmot Basin Road.)

2. In about 300 m turn left onto Centennial Trail (also Mt. Allan ski trail), which once was an access trail to an open pit coal mine. Keep straight a little way in. At the next intersection around a bend, turn left up the fall line. (Straight on is the ski trail.)

3. The going is steep. After a while you cross in close succession five intersecting "truck-driven roads" on their way to Mine Scar, as the mine is now called after revegetation. Cross the first (lowest). At the second go right then continue up. Cross the third (Coal Mine ski trail). At the fourth turn left, then take the second road to the right that winds up the hill. At the fifth cross then keep right. Now you're set.

4. Switchback up a grassy rib, enjoying the views that are unfolding of Ribbon Creek valley. Take a breather on a shoulder, then zig some more up a shaley slope to the apex of three grass ribs—the start of the Centennial Ridge proper.

Mt. Allan. The trail follows the grassy rib starting from a third of the way up the right-hand side of the picture. Olympic Summit is the grassy top just to the right of the orange shale summit.

5. Walk to the upcoming rock step. It looks alarming but is easily turned on the right (north) side by a series of broad ledges and a gully that calls for hands in a few places. From the top it's an easy walk to the grassy top of Olympic Summit which is decorated by weather instruments.

6. Disconcertingly, the ridge descends. Start uphill again, winding through the "Mushroom Garden," itself only a prelude to the spectacular passage between the rocky ridge crest and a row of 25 m-high conglomerate pinnacles. A little down-scrambling in another rock garden brings you to the final section of ridge.

7. This is a straightforward climb on orange shale and screes. Although it is not necessary to do so, most hikers follow the trail along the left slope just below the crest. High up the trail circles around to the north ridge and misses out the summit completely. So tackle the final rise to the summit cairn direct.

8. The view is dominated by the nearby much higher peaks of Mt. Lougheed and Wind Mountain.

Above: Starting up the zigzags of the initial grass ridge at 4. In the background is Mt. Kidd. Photo Tony Daffern.

Below: Looking from the apex of three ridges to the rock step at 5. The trail follows ledges on the shady right side.

Above: Looking from Olympic Summit to the top of Mt. Allan, still a long way distant. A third of the way along you catch a glimpse of the Mushroom Garden and the pinnacles. To left rises the much higher Wind Mountain and the peaks of Mt. Lougheed.

Right: Weather instruments on top of Olympic Summit. In the background are the two summits of Mt. Colembola.

Above: Passing two of the pinnacles, between 6 and 7. In the background is Ribbon Peak and Mt. Bogart. Photo Tony Daffern.

Right: Looking back at Olympic Summit and the pinnacles from the last stretch of ridge rising to the summit.

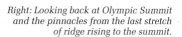

The summit is dwarfed by the nearby peaks of Mt. Lougheed. Photo Tony Daffern.

The trail was built by the Rocky Mountain Ramblers as a centennial project starting in 1966 and took three years to complete. Look for a plaque at the rock gardens on your return.

11 Ribbon Falls

Distance 16.4 km return
Height gain 311 m
High point 1800 m
Easy
Late spring, summer, fall

Start: Hwy. 40 (Kananaskis Trail). Turn west onto the road to Nakiska Ski Area (Mt. Allan Drive). Turn first left onto Centennial Drive, then next right onto Ribbon Creek Road. Drive to the far end parking lot (picnic shelter, picnic tables, biffy).

Difficulty: Good well-marked trail with easy grades. Later the trail narrows and is more undulating. All river crossings are bridged.

A long and easy trail follows a valley hemmed in by cliffs to an impressive waterfall. By biking to the end of the logging road portion you can reduce the walk to 8.4 km return. Going beyond the waterfall is for scramblers only.

1. The Ribbon Creek Trail (logging road from the 1940s) leaves the far end of the parking lot between interpretive signs, and heads into a meadow. Soon you enter the valley confines, winding under high banks alongside the always boisterous creek. Cross two bridges. Back on the north bank, you pass picnic tables en route to a signposted junction. Keep straight. (To left Link ski trail descends and bridges the creek.)

2. Continue through spruce forest, noting skid trails and loading ramps to the right. Close to the north fork is an unmarked junction with the Memorial Lakes trail. Stay straight on the logging road and cross the bridge over the north fork.

3. Just beyond is a small meadow with picnic table, former site of Eau Claire Lumber Company's on site accommodation and office. Here the valley turns southwest and is enclosed by the high cliffs of Ribbon

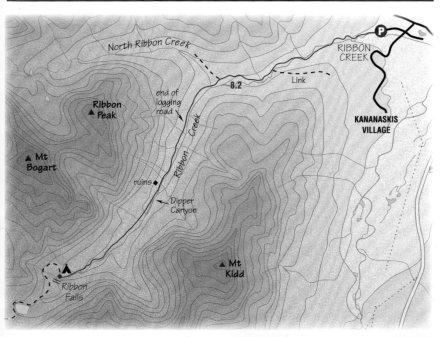

Peak and Mt. Kidd for the rest of the way. The logging road section ends in a half kilometre at a bike rack.

4. Carrying on along the right bank is a rolling single-track trail. You cross a few side creeks, then at the start of the canyon climb onto a bench. Watch for the ruins of log cabins left over from earlier logging days. Shortly after, traverse steeper slopes above "Dipper Canyon", two delightful sections of river with alternating falls and plunge pools. The river then calms down a bit and the valley opens out below large avalanche slopes. The trail is mainly flat with a few small uphills to Ribbon Falls backcountry campground.

5. Climb farther up the trail to two benches overlooking Ribbon Falls, which is worth every metre of the slog in.

Left: Starting along the trail from Ribbon Creek parking lot. In the background is Ribbon Peak.

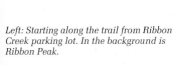

The second bridge over Ribbon Creek. Photo Tony Daffern.

Top and above: Dipper Canyon. Photos Jim Bell and Roy Millar.

Left: Ribbon Falls.

The trail continues above the falls, eventually reaching Ribbon Lake. However, it is an exposed scramble up cliffs where you must pull yourself up using chains.

12 Lillian Lake

Distance 13 km Lillian Lake
Height gain 500 m
High point 2030 m
Moderately strenuous
Summer, fall
Opens July 1

A hike up scenic Galatea Creek to a popular fishing and camping lake. A must-do option is to continue further to two blue tarns in the alpine meadows.

Start: From the Trans-Canada Highway (Hwy. 1), drive 32.4 km south on Hwy. 40 (Kananaskis Trail) to the Galatea day-use area.

Difficulty: A good well-marked trail to Lillian Lake with occasional loose tread. In places the grade is moderately steep, especially toward the end. All creek crossings are bridged.

1. From the parking lot descend a wide gravel trail to the suspension bridge over the Kananaskis River and cross it. Shortly the trail bridges Galatea Creek to a T-junction. Turn left. (To right is Terrace Trail.)

2. After an up-down, you arrive at the narrows where the trail bridges the turbulent creek four times.

3. On the north bank the trail crosses a couple of stoney runnels, then undulates high across the south slopes of Mt. Kidd, crossing avalanche paths and strips of meadow. Down left, the creek is enclosed in a gorge. Descend to cross bridge #5.

4. A flat walk through spruce forest ends at the forks. Cross bridge #6 and start up the northwest fork.

5. The initial stretch along the right bank is easy through long grass meadows. Then the trail crosses to the left bank and what follows is a long sustained climb through forest to a T-junction at the bottom of an avalanche slope. Keep straight. (To right is Guinns Pass Trail.)

6. After more uphill, the trail levels in the vicinity of Lillian Lake. The trail crosses the outlet and runs along the north shore to a junction. Stay left by the lake. (The trail to right, signed "Galatea Lakes," leads to the biffy.)

7. Continue along the shoreline to the backcountry campground at the west end. Swimming is popular in the lake's shallow green waters.

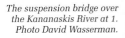

The suspension bridge over the Kananaskis River at 1. Photo David Wasserman.

Left: The trail at 3 traversing meadows above the canyon. In the background is The Wedge.

Below: Lillian Lake, looking toward the avalanche slopes of the west end. The campground is located in the trees at right.

Going farther to Galatea Lakes

Distance 3 km return
Height gain 190 m

The trail is fair, the initial steep grade moderating to easy. Expect much scree with cairns marking the trail. Some route finding may be needed.

1. Start at the biffy or from the trail that leaves from halfway along the lakeshore.

2. The trail crosses a dry draw, then climbs the headwall to the left of a scree slope. When the ground levels wend left across scree using cairns. Between you and Lower Galatea Lake is a low ridge. At a junction with an older trail keep right up scree (cairn) and traverse through a gap at the right side of the ridge. Down below you lies the lower lake in a rock-girt bowl.

3. To reach Upper Galatea Lake, continue traversing above the north shore. Between the two lakes is another low ridge. The trail descends to the west shore then climbs to a gap on the left side of the ridge. In the gap is a 4-way junction. Go straight. (To left is a trail come up the harder, steeper way from the campground. To right a trail heads out along the ridge top—a good viewpoint.)

4. The trail, fast losing definition, descends meadows to Upper Galatea Lake.

5. It's best to return the same way.

At Galatea Lakes you'll find this unusual white version of the penstemon commonly called Creeping beardtongue.

Lower Galatea Lake from the ridge between the lakes.

The deep blue waters of Lower Galatea Lake. Looking toward the ridge between the two lakes and a mountain known as The Tower.

The blue-green waters of Upper Galatea Lake.

13 *Upper Kananaskis Lake*

Distance 16 km loop
Height gain 60 m
High point 1783 m
Easy
Summer, fall

A circumnavigation of the lake at the heart of K Country. Once "a revelation of beauty hardly equalled anywhere," the lake is now a reservoir.

Start: From Hwy. 40 turn west onto Kananaskis Lakes Trail and follow it to its end at North Interlakes parking lot. You can also start from Upper Lake parking lot en route: Stay left, keep right and turn next right into parking lots nearest the lake. For south shore trail, turn left and drive to the far end. For east shore trail turn right.

Difficulty: Good well-marked trails. One section is over rocks with steps. Grades are mostly flat or undulating. All creek crossings are bridged.

1. Walk down to the trailhead kiosk on the shore of Upper Kananaskis Lake.

2. Follow Three Isle Lake Trail along the isthmus and cross the intake pipe by bridge. Swing left onto the fire road. Keep straight. (To right is the unsigned Indefatigable trail.) Turn next left off the fire road onto Upper Kananaskis Lake Trail.

3 The trail runs along the north shore to a T-junction. Keep left. (To right is a connector trail to the fire road.) The trail climbs into the blinding glare of a huge boulder field where steps facilitate passage across its humps and hollows.

4. At a T-junction keep right. (To left is the spur trail to Point backcountry campground located on a peninsula.)

5. Pass a green tarn, then contour around the head of a deep inlet. Turn up the east bank of the Kananaskis River, stopping awhile at a bench to admire Lower Kananaskis Falls. Cross the river above the falls and in a couple of minutes reach an unsigned junction. Keep straight. (To right is the decommissioned Lyautey trail.)

6. The west shore section undulates through deep forest with no views. At the mid point keep straight at an unsigned junction. (To right is the Hidden Lake-Aster Lake trail for scramblers only.)

Club group at the trailhead kiosk.

Unnamed mountain reflected in the bay near the trailhead.

The trail in the extensive boulderfield at 3. Called the Palliser Slide, it is the result of two catastrophic landslides off Mt. Indefatigable. Photo Allan Cole.

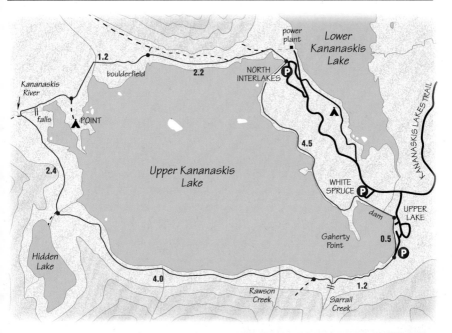

7. The trail drops to the lakeshore at an islet and stays there for the rest of the way to Upper Lake parking lots. It's a long lonely stretch along the south shore but finally you come to a T-junction. Keep straight. (To right is Rawson Lake Trail.) Then cross Sarrail Creek below a waterfall. One final kilometre and you arrive at the southernmost Upper Lake parking lot.

8. Walk through to the northernmost parking lot where the trail continues. Cross a bridge at interpretive signs, then cross the boat launch road onto Upper Lake Dam and cross it. At dam's end keep left. (To right is a trail come up from White Spruce parking lot.)

9. Cross a grassy "bay." In the trees following stay on the main trail. (Side trail to left leads to Gaherty's Point.) Reach the windy east shore with its gravel beaches and great views and turn north.

10. The trail runs below hilly Interlakes Peninsula, winding in and out of bays, finally rounding a headland back to the trailhead.

Lower Kananaskis Falls at 5.

Left: View from the west shore at 7, looking across at Mt. Indefatigable.

Centre: The Opal Range at sunset from the south shore at 8.

Bottom: Typical view along the east shore at 10. In the background are mounts Foch and Sarrail. Still in evidence is the damage done during enlargement of the lake over 50 years ago. Pre reservoir there were many more islands and promontories and Upper Lake Dam was the site of the beautiful Twin Falls between the lakes.

14 *Rawson Lake*

Distance 7.8 km return
Height gain 310 m
High point 2030 m
Moderate
Summer, fall

Start: From Kananaskis Trail (Hwy. 40) turn west onto Kananaskis Lakes Trail and follow it to Upper Lake parking lot access road. Stay left, keep right and turn right. At the T-junction turn left and drive to the far end of the parking lot.

Difficulty: A good well-marked trail with a moderately steep grade.

A beautiful green lake in a cirque. Grizzlies are occasionally sighted on the meadows above the lake.

Setting out on Upper Kananaskis Lake Trail at 1.

1. From Upper Lake parking lot head along the south shore section of Upper Kananaskis Lake Trail. The trail winding in and out of every indentation of the shoreline is quite rolling. Cross Sarrail Creek below the waterfall and in 100 m come to a T-junction. Turn left onto Rawson Lake Trail.

2. All too soon the trail starts zigzagging uphill through old spruce forest. It's a moderately steep climb that levels off half a kilometre before the lake. Your first view of the lake backdropped by Mt. Sarrail is from the outlet. The trail continues along the southeast shore to strips of meadow where it officially ends at an interpretive sign. En route you pass a biffy.

3. A rougher trail can be followed along the rocky shoreline to the far west end.

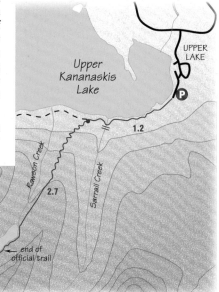

Sarrail Falls on Upper Kananaskis Lake Trail is a popular stopping place.

Not the usual view of Rawson Lake. This photo was taken from the far end at 3 looking back. The main trail ends on the patch of grass at centre left.

15 *Indefatigable Trail*

Distance 4.4 km return
Height gain 503 m
High point 2225 m
Strenuous
Summer, fall

*Everybody's favourite trail.
Views of both Kananaskis lakes
will have you reaching for your
camera at every twist and turn.*

Start: From Kananaskis Trail (Hwy. 40) turn west onto Kananaskis Lakes Trail and follow it to the end at North Interlakes day-use area.

Difficulty: Generally a good trail with one steep section where the trail is eroded and the footing either loose on shale or slabby. Occasional grizzly sightings in the meadows.

NOTE In 2005 this most popular of popular trails was demoted to unofficial status, reasons cited including trail erosion and frequency of bear closures. All signs, interpretive trails and benches were removed.

1. Walk down to the trailhead kiosk on the shore of Upper Kananaskis Lake.

2. Follow Three Isle Lake trail along the isthmus and cross the intake pipe by bridge. Swing left onto the fire road and almost straightaway turn right onto Indefatigable trail. It can be identified by rocks strewn across the entrance.

3. After easy windings in forest, the trail and variations climb up the left side of a rocky ridge. Near the top veer right onto the ridge crest, gained at the Wendy Elekes Viewpoint. The View of Upper Kananaskis Lake is superlative.

4. After a dip, continue more easily up the ridge on the edge of an eastern escarpment. To right is Lower Kananaskis Lake.

5. The trail levels and reaches its high point where two single-track trails turn off to the left. Keep right and descending slightly, continue to the end of the main trail. From here is a view of the outlier climbed in Going Farther.

*Climbing up the rocky ridge at 3
below the viewpoint.*

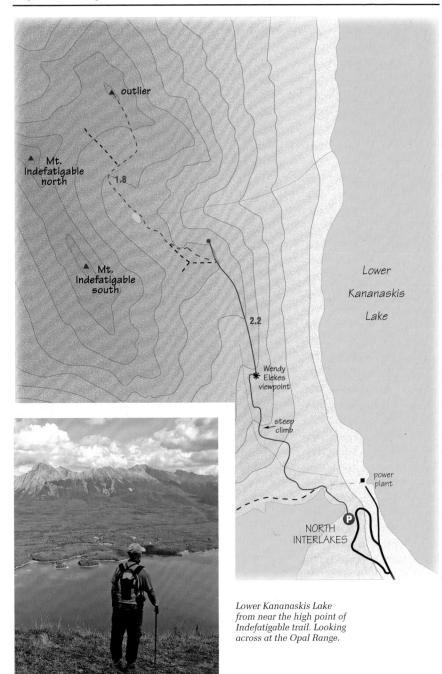

outlier

Mt.
Indefatigable
north

1.8

Mt.
Indefatigable
south

Lower

Kananaskis

Lake

2.2

Wendy
Elekes
viewpoint

steep
climb

power
plant

NORTH
INTERLAKES

Lower Kananaskis Lake
from near the high point of
Indefatigable trail. Looking
across at the Opal Range.

Upper Kananaskis Lake from the Wendy Elekes Viewpoint.

Going farther to the outlier

Distance add on 3.6 km return
Height gain 260 m
High point 2484 m

The high point of the eastern escarpment offers yet another view to the north. An unmarked single track trail, easy at first, ends with a moderately steep pull up grass and scree to the top.

1. At Indefatigable's high point turn second left. The trail climbs into larch forest with glades of Glacier lilies. Keep right at the next junction.

2. Traverse steep hillside into a hanging valley occupied by a seasonal tarn. Turn it on the right shore. In season the meadows hereabouts are crammed with flowers.

3. The trail climbs curving right through last trees to a junction. Keep straight. (Trail to left climbs to the col between the outlier and Mt. Indefatigable north.)

4. On reaching the south ridge of the outlier the trail turns left and more or less follows the ridge crest on grass, then scree. Just below the summit stay well back from the escarpment edge.

Grizzly digging near the seasonal pond.

65

Left: The seasonal pond in the hanging valley at O2. After rounding the pond, the trail climbs through trees and glades just to the right of the centre draw. Unseen in this photo, it then makes for the right-hand skyline ridge which is followed up to the summit at top right.

Above: On the grassy south ridge at the start of the scree. In the background is Lower Kananaskis Lake, Highwood Pass at left and Elk Pass at right.

Left: The summit of Indefatigable Outlier at the crumbling edge of the eastern escarpment.

16 *Ptarmigan Cirque*

Distance 3.6 km return
Height gain 230 m
High point 2438 m
Moderate
Summer, fall

A short hike to a typical alpine cirque where you can linger all day. Alpine flowers, fossils and ptarmigan are just some of the interesting things to be seen.

Start: Hwy. 40 (Kananaskis Trail) at Highwood Pass parking lot. This stretch of road is open from June 16 to November 30.

Difficulty: A good well-marked interpretive trail with a moderately easy switchbacks into the cirque. Two minor creek crossings. Occasionally closed after grizzly sightings.

1. At the trail sign follow a trail over a bridge into Highwood Pass meadows.

2. Stay on the main trail. (To left is a single track trail to Pocaterra Tarn.) At the next junction fork right. (Ahead is Highwood Pass Meadows Interpretive Trail.) Then cross the highway at the high point of the pass.

The trail at 1 in meadows near the parking lot. The pass is the highest navigable road in Canada.

3. The trails zigs back and forth through fir and spruce forest.

4. Keep straight at a T-junction with the return loop. The trail wanders across alpine meadows back-dropped by the cliffs of Little Arethusa.

5. Keep right. (To left a secondary trail continues up the cirque and is used by scramblers climbing Mt. Rae.)

6. The interpretive trail crosses the creek above a small waterfall.

7. The trail turns down creek, winding through rocks and small patches of meadow, eventually recrossing the creek above a small waterfall.

8. Come to the T-junction with the loop trail and turn left, returning the same way you came up.

Crossing the creek at the turnaround point at 6. In the background is the lower summit of Mt. Rae "The Pinnacle," which is connected to Mt. Arethusa by King's Ridge.

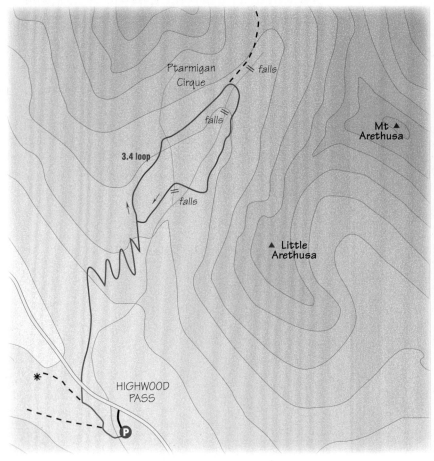

Yellow and white flower gardens at 4.

Dwarf Mountain Groundsel.

Below the cliffs of Little Arethusa at 4.

From 6 looking back toward Mt. Tyrwhitt.

17 Pocaterra Tarn

Distance 4.2 km return
Height gain 204 m
High point 2235 m
Moderate to tarn
Summer, fall

Start: Kananaskis Trail (Hwy. 40) at Highwood Pass parking lot. This stretch of road is open June 16 to November 30.

Difficulty: Fairly good trail with moderate grades. The longest steepest uphills are on the return. Occasionally mud and loose rocks. Minor creek crossings.

A walk through mature spruce forest to a small tarn. Larch meadows invite further exploration.

1. From the parking lot cross the footbridge onto Highwood Pass Meadows Interpretive Trail. Shortly turn left onto an unsigned single track trail. There may be a sign saying stay on the trail through the meadow.

2. The trail follows a grassy draw (old river channel) to a boulder at the left edge and heads into the trees.

3. Shortly cross a tiny creek and climb up the right side of it through a damp forest of spruce where the trail may be muddy. Around the first high point ignore three minor trails heading up left.

4. The trail rises below a rock to a second high point, then makes a long twisting descent with occasional steep shaley drops.

5. Level out and cross a lush avalanche slope. The trail climbs a little, then descend in zigs to a fork of Pocaterra Creek.

6. Climb up the left bank, then cross to the right bank shortly before the creek goes underground below rubble.

7. Come to Pocaterra Tarn, located between scree slopes and larch meadows.

Larches fringe Pocaterra Tarn. In the background are mounts Rae and Arethusa.

In summer the scree slopes above the tarn are pink with Mountain fireweed.

The meadows of upper Pocaterra Creek at O1. In the background rises the 4th top of Pocaterra Ridge. If you're not going to Grizzly Col, it's worth coming this far just for a wander by the creek.

At O2, en route to the cirque which is around the corner to the left. Ahead is Mt. Tyrwhitt. Its wishbone arch is seen halfway up the left-hand skyline ridge.

Going farther to Grizzly Col

Distance add 3.6 km return
Height gain add 385 m
High point 2620 m

A scrambler's access trail to Mt. Tyrwhitt. Go as far as you feel able to: Wander the larch meadows alongside the creek, climb into the cirque or tackle the trail to the col. The terrain gets progressively rougher as you go on, ending with a steep side slope of scree that may still have snow patches in mid summer. A little route-finding may be necessary. Grades remain easy to moderate.

The cirque at O4. The trail can be seen rising from left to right to the col.

1. From the tarn the trail continues up rocks at the edge of the trees, then heads right into flat meadows alongside Pocaterra Creek. At a T-junction keep straight. (Trail to right leads to Little Highwood Pass.)

2. The trail rises and falls to another junction. Keep left. (Trail to right is another trail to Little Highwood Pass.) En route look for the arch on Mt. Tyrwhitt.

3. The climb into the cirque is easy. You follow a draw between hillside and a wall of moraine on the right. When this ends you transfer into an upper draw, but not for long. Shortly the trail climbs up the left bank and along a terrace. Just past a cairn it appears to peter out. Turn sharp left uphill.

4. Shortly the trail reasserts itself. It climbs uphill at a moderate grade, then turns right into a long rising traverse of a deepening scree slope to the col between Mt. Tyrwhitt and an unnamed ridge to the east.

5. Ahead lies the west fork of Storm Creek. The best view is back toward Little Highwood Pass.

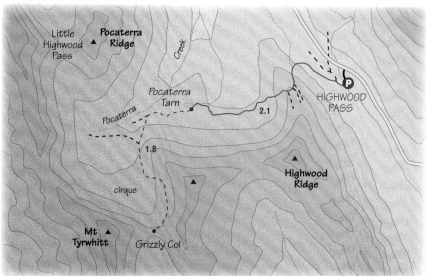

The trail at O5 crosses a steep side slope of scree to the col. Snow earlier in the summer can make the going tricky.

Grizzly Col, showing a very foreshortened view of Mt. Tyrwhitt. By wandering up the grassy ridge to the left you get a much truer perspective of the col and the mountain.

18 *South Buller Pass*

Distance 13.4 km return
Height gain 671 m
High point 2484 m
Moderately strenuous
Summer, fall

*A high pass in the Kananaskis
Range with a million dollar
view of Ribbon Lake.*

Start: Hwy. 742 (Smith-Dorrien-Spray Trail) at Buller Mountain day-use area.

Difficulty: A well-marked trail with occasional steep sections. Near the end switchbacks on scree and slippery shale. All creek crossings are bridged.

1. Walk out to the highway and cross it. The trail starts from the east side of the highway opposite the access road.

2. The trail makes a beeline for Buller Creek and crosses it. Climb steadily along the northwest bank under Mt. Buller to a flat of Engelmann spruce where the creek is re-crossed to the southeast bank.

3. Coming up is the hard work of the day, a prolonged twisting climb up a step in the valley floor. At the top traverse left back to the creek and pass a waterfall splashing into a circular pool. Top-up the water bottles from the creek above.

4. Descend slightly to the forks. The trail crosses the south fork to a junction. Turn right. (Left is the less well-defined north pass trail.)

5. The trail follows the arid south fork between ridges of grey stones. Fast time to be made to the foot of the headwall as the valley floor is amazingly wide and flat, and covered in grass.

6. The climb up the headwall is the second big climb of the day. Climb scree up the left side, then make a long traverse right above a slabby area, the angle moderating as you turn left onto the pass. A large cairn marks the high point. Ahead is a million dollar view of Ribbon Lake backdropped by the two peaks of Mt. Kidd.

Top, left and right:
Fleabane meadows
near treeline.

Right: The trail up the
south fork at 5. The low
point in the background is
South Buller Pass.

Left: The waterfall at 3, at
the top of the climb from
the valley floor.

Looking up at the pass from the end of 5. The trail can be seen traversing from left to right.

A hiker descending from the pass into the start of the traverse at 6.

Looking back from the pass down the south fork of Buller Creek. To left is Mt. Engadine. Mt. Assiniboine can be spotted in the far distance at right.

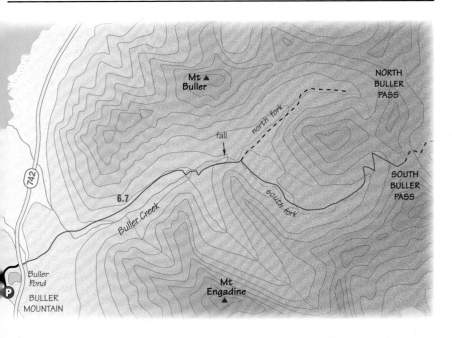

The million dollar view of Ribbon Lake from the pass.
Rising above the lake are the two peaks of Mt. Kidd.

19 Burstall Pass

Distance 15 km return
Height gain 472 m
High point 2380 m
Moderately strenuous
Summer, fall

Start: Hwy. 742 (Smith-Dorrien-Spray Trail) at Burstall Pass parking lot.

Difficulty: Overall a good well-marked trail. On the alluvial flat the route is marked with posts and you can expect to do some icy-cold paddling. Grades are moderately easy with one steep haul up the headwall above the flat. Remnant snow is likely in early summer.

1. From the parking lot head out on a trail that crosses Mud Lake dam. Note the canal on the left side transporting Burstall Creek water into the Smith-Dorrien Creek system. In the open, the trail—now reverted to logging road—wends left to an unsigned junction. Keep left. (The logging road to right leads to Hogarth Lakes.)

2. Climb a hill to the next junction and turn right. (The logging road ahead is the route followed up French Creek to the Haig Icefield.)

A long approach along a logging road, then trail, gains you the cheerful green and white karst country of alpine meadows. By biking to the end of the logging road, the hiking can be cut down to 9.2 km.

3. In spruce forest, the Burstall Creek logging road settles into a long gentle climb past numerous skid trails you are unlikely to mistake for the trail. To your right Burstall Creek is out of sight in a canyon. After the grade levels, keep straight at a T-junction. (To right a logging road crosses Burstall Creek—no bridge—to join with the Hogarth Lakes roads.)

4. The road continues fairly flat with one uphill, travelling below avalanche slopes on the left, and Burstall Lakes on the right. The three lakes can't be seen from the road and are hardly worth the effort of a detour, being muddy coloured. The logging road ends at bike locks.

5. A trail continues, heading downhill to a bridge over Burstall Creek. Enter a large alluvial flat where the way forward is marked with red markers on posts. Shortly, cross the flat below the Robertson Glacier, the source of all the stones and wandering glacial streams that defeat any attempts at bridge building. This is where you may have to paddle a braid or two. Look left for a view of the glacier slung between mounts Robertson and Sir Douglas. The good trail resumes in trees to the left of the avalanche slope.

6. A steep twisty climb up the timbered headwall gains you the big flat meadow below Birdwood Pass. To your right is Mount Birdwood.

Left: Mud Lake from the dam at 1. Its unattractive grey colour results from debris brought down by the Robertson Glacier.

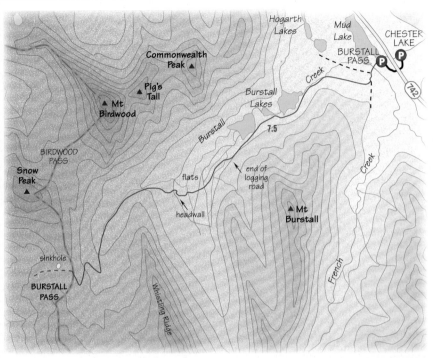

Above: When you cross the flats at 5, look left for a view of the Robertson Glacier between Mt. Robertson (left) and Mt. Sir Douglas. In winter the glacier is a popular ski destination.

Right: The trail up the headwall at 6. Photo David Wasserman.

79

7. Cross the meadow to the mouth of a draw. The trail resumes climbing, more easily this time, up the right bank through trees and flowery glades.

8. The ground levels momentarily at treeline. Ahead is a barren karst landscape of rock scattered with clumps of spruce and larch. Glaciated Mt. Sir Douglas is just starting to poke up above the horizon. At a post the main trail turns right. (The trail ahead leads toward South Burstall Pass, a more distant objective.)

9. In the final climb, the trail heads up through a few trees onto a rocky crest, zigs left, then right, approaching Burstall Pass from the south. A signpost marks the spot.

Right: At 6 you cross the flat meadow below Mt. Birdwood.

Below: The trail ascends the verdant valley at bottom left to Burstall Pass at right centre. In the distance Mt. Sir Douglas rises above South Burstall Pass.

Top: Whistling Ridge from the pass. Photo David Wasserman.

Centre: Reaching Burstall Pass. In the background are Mt. Birdwood, Pig's Tail and Commonwealth Peak.

Right: Beautiful Leman Lake from the viewpoint west of the pass.

20 *Chester Lake*

Distance 10.2 km return
Height gain 310 m to lake
High point 2220 m at lake
Moderate
Summer, fall

Start: Hwy. 742 (Smith-Dorrien-Spray Trail) at Chester Lake parking lot.

Difficulty: Well-marked trails through-out. Moderate climb on logging roads, followed by a short steep section on trail, then easy grades to the lake. Creeks are bridged.

A moderately easy hike through forest and meadows to a jade-coloured lake in the larch belt. By biking to the end of the logging roads, the hiking is reduced to 4.8 km.

1. The logging road leaves the top end of the parking lot near the biffy. Pass through a gate to a junction. Turn left. (Right is upper Blue ski trail.)

2. Cross a bridge over Chester Creek. At the next junction turn right. Between here and the next signpost at the 5-way junction the main logging road is obvious, taking every uphill option. You aren't likely to stray onto any overgrown skid trail. At the 5-way junction with sign, turn right. (To left is the ski route to Chester Lake.)

3. After a straight the logging road turns uphill (sign), then turns right into a long traverse. Bike racks indicate the end of the logging road section.

4. Head left up a narrow, twisty trail into a forest of spruce and fir. After the grade levels you alternate between forest and hummocky meadows. At the second meadow the ski trail comes in from the left.

5. The trail climbs a little, then levels again and you enter the big meadow that extends right across the creek which is now bubbling away to your right.

6. Arrive at the lake, overlooked by the cliffs of Mt. Chester. Here the trail splits, one trail bridging the outlet into a larch clump and pica rockpile, the other following the west shoreline.

7. On the west shoreline the trail again splits. The better-used trail heads across a ridge into Three Lakes Valley, the other climbs into the upper valley under The Fortress.

Near the end of the logging road section at 3 is this view looking back to mounts French, Robertson and Sir Douglas.

The last big meadow before the lake at 5. The prominent peak to left is unnamed. To right are the cliffs of Mt. Chester. Photo David Wasserman.

Chester Lake from the west shore.

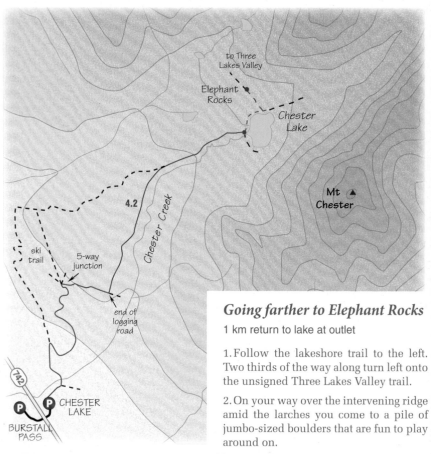

to Three
Lakes Valley

Elephant
Rocks

Chester
Lake

Mt
Chester

4.2

Chester Creek

ski
trail

5-way
junction

end of
logging
road

742

P P CHESTER
LAKE

BURSTALL
PASS

Going farther to Elephant Rocks

1 km return to lake at outlet

1. Follow the lakeshore trail to the left. Two thirds of the way along turn left onto the unsigned Three Lakes Valley trail.

2. On your way over the intervening ridge amid the larches you come to a pile of jumbo-sized boulders that are fun to play around on.

Elephant Rocks.

21 Headwall Lakes

Distance 13.6 km upper lake return
Height gain 451 m to upper lake
High point 2341 m
Moderately strenuous
Summer, fall

Start: Hwy. 742 (Smith-Dorrien-Spray Trail) at Chester Lake parking lot.

Difficulty: Trail varies from good, well-marked colour-coded logging roads (ski trails) to a fair trail that is rough in places with scree underfoot. Grades also vary between easy to steep. The one creek crossing is bridged.

A valley containing all the finest components of mountain scenery: climax forest, blue lakes, waterfalls, meadows, and karst pavement. By biking the logging road section you cut the hiking down to 6.4 km.

Yellow ski trail (logging road) at 4, near where you leave it for the Headwall Lakes trail.

1. From the biffy follow lower Blue ski trail that runs along the bank top above the parking lot and into the trees. The trail descends slightly, then unexpectedly turns sharp left up a steep hill. At the top it turns back right and meanders through a miniature valley to a T-junction with a wider logging road that is coded yellow. Turn left on blue/yellow.

2. A long winding uphill leads to a junction. Keep right on Yellow. (To left is upper Blue logging road/ski trail.)

3. Continue climbing to a logged area on a broad ridge and curve left. At a junction go straight. (To left is Orange ski trail.)

4. The going is level to Headwall Creek bridge. Then the road climbs and zigs right, the gradient easing off at a cutblock on the left side. Here you leave the logging road and turn left on a single-track trail.

5. A fairly level stint through spruce forest brings you back to Headwall Creek. The trail continues along the right bank, through willows, then through more forest, and ultimately below a scree slope.

6. Barely back in forest, the trail starts a steep twisting climb to treeline. At the top the trail turns left and in two traverses separated by a small step, arrives below the first headwall, a white wall of rock. A climb up the right side on scree gains you the top. Underfoot is a fascinating karst pavement. Below lies Lower Headwall Lake in a rock-girt bowl.

7. The trail follows the right shoreline, initially on grass, then across scree (use the upper trail). Ahead is a second headwall covered in grass. The trail climbs up the right side of the tumbling stream that spouts out of the hillside at three-quarter height. From the top it's a short walk to Upper Headwall Lake which has a very austere setting under The Fortress.

The trail at 6 leading to the first headwall.

Karst pavement above the first headwall at 6.

Beautiful Lower Headwall Lake. To the right of the waterfall you can see the trail climbing the second headwall to the upper lake.

*Lower Headwall Lake from near the top of the second headwall.
Through the vee are the peaks of the Spray Mountains.*

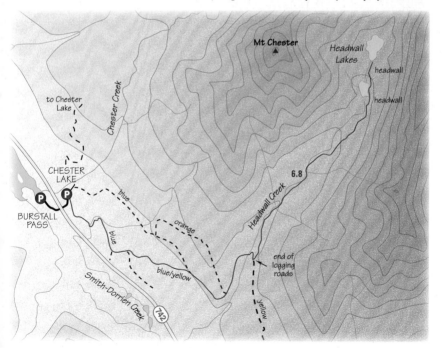

*Left: The stream
gushing out of the
hillside at 7.
Photo Peter Snell.*

*Below: The austere setting of Upper Headwall Lake. At the head of the valley rises
The Fortress which is usually climbed from the head of the valley via its left-hand ridge.*

22 Mist Ridge

Distance 18.4 km south summit return
Height gain 655 m to south summit
High point 2423 m
Moderately strenuous
Summer after June 15, fall

Start: Hwy. 40 (Kananaskis Trail) at Mist Creek day-use area.

Difficulty: Initially, a very good well-marked trail followed by a good un-marked trail (exploration road) that leads onto Mist Ridge with one minor creek crossing. On the ridge itself the trail is poor on grass with rock.

A long approach up valleys to the south summit of Mist Ridge. One of K Country's premier ridgewalks.

1. Start off on Mist Creek Trail that heads north from the parking lot to the highway. Cross just right of the Mist Creek culvert.

2. At a T-junction with the old highway a few metres in, turn right, then almost immediately left into forest. While signposted as "Mist Creek Trail," your trail is actually a coal exploration road. It kicks off with two easy uphills separated by a flat boggy meadow. After it levels out you come to a T-junction with sign. Turn right up the exploration road. (The trail ahead is Mist Creek Trail up the main valley.)

3. The road climbs along the right slope of the east fork. At a T-junction keep straight. (The road to right leads to a col then onto the lower slopes of ridges on both sides.)

4. Unexpectedly the road drops in two zigs to the valley bottom. Cross a side creek (last water) and start the climb over again. Long zigs take you out of the trees into the meadows to a col where you're treated to a view of Gibraltar Mountain. Continue uphill and left to a second col with a fabulous view of Mist Mountain.

5. Here is a T-junction. Straight is the road continued which soon ends. Right is a nebulous horse trail that cuts out the South Summit by a traverse of the left (west) flank. Go neither way. Simply walk up an easy grass slope to the south end of the south summit.

6. Continue along the narrowish rocky crest to its high point for a view of the rest of the ridge.

7. Return the same way or try the option.

The T-junction at 4. Looking across Mist Creek to the Misty Range.

At 4, looking back along the grassy exploration road from near its end below the South Summit. In the background rise unnamed summits of the Highwood Range.

Looking back at the south summit from the ridge to the north. The trail can be seen descending to the col. From the col a nebulous horse trail traverses the right-hand slopes to the exploration road.

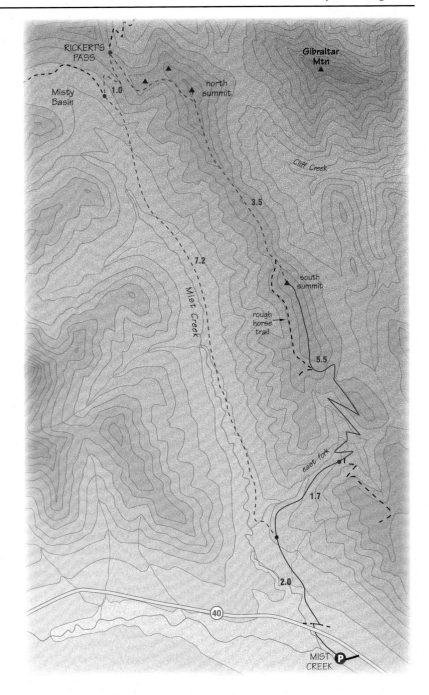

Going farther all along the ridge

Distance 22.9 km loop
Height gain 890 m from trailhead
High point 2515 m

A beautiful ridgewalk to Rickert's Pass with a return down Mist Creek. Trails range from poor on the ridge with occasional scree and rock to a very good marked trail down the valley. Route-finding may be needed. Owing to the greater distance and height gain, the route upgrades to strenuous.

1. The trail descends moderately steeply to a col, a crossroads of sheep trails.

2. After a bit of undulating, the ridge narrows and rises ruler-straight over a series of false tops to the highest North Summit of Mist Ridge. Follow either the rocky crest or the trail on the left side. Below the actual summit the trail turns off down the left-hand slope. Ignore it temporarily and climb to the summit cairn.

3. Continue on (or not) to the northernmost summit, which entails an easy scramble up a rock band. Return to the trail and turn right.

4. The trail makes a gradually descending traverse of the steep and stoney west flank to a col. Now heading west, it further descends and contours well below the westernmost summit on the meadows of the south slope. Again, this rocky top is rarely visited.

5. Arrive at a viewpoint on a promontory overlooking Misty Basin. Here the trail improves and you follow it out below the grassy ridge crest into a rocky defile that is Rickert's Pass. At the unsigned T-junction turn left onto Mist Creek Trail.

6. The trail zigs down through flowery meadows into the fir forest of Mist Valley. En route keep straight. (A side trail to right leads to Misty Basin.)

7. For the next 7 km good time can be made along the left bank of Mist Creek. The going is flat and easy through forest, with occasional tiny creeks to cross. A steep descent brings you to the east fork. Cross on rocks, then wind up a hill to the T-junction with your outgoing route. Keep straight and return the same way you came up.

View from the North Summit to the northernmost top with rockband at O3.

A rocky section of ridge at O2 where the trail takes to the left slope.

Above: From the col at O4, looking back at the descending trail from the North Summit at right.

Right: The westernmost summit that is often missed out by a traverse of the left flank. In the background Storm Mountain rises above Misty Basin.

Left: At O2 the ridge rises over a number of tops to the North Summit at right.

23 Picklejar Lakes

Distance 10 km to 4th lake return
Height gain 615 m
High point 2190 m
Moderate
Summer after June 15, fall

Start: Hwy. 40 (Kananaskis Trail) at Lantern Creek day-use area.

Difficulty: A good trail with loose footing on shale and scree about the pass. Trails around the lakes are occasionally indistinct where they cross rocks. Grades also vary. Here and there grades are moderately steep, particularly on the south side of the pass where care is needed. Route-finding may be necessary around the lakes where there are myriad trails.

1. From the parking lot cross the highway and walk left a short way. After crossing Lantern Creek turn right on a trail that heads along the left bank of the creek.

A climb over a grassy pass to four lakes located in an alpine basin.

2. After a preliminary section of gaining height slowly through trees, the trail seesaws across steep grassy hillsides, finally levelling out in trees for a spell. A brief up/down in a meadow precedes the crossing of the tiny north fork of Lantern Creek.

3. Start the climb to the pass. A short stint through trees precedes the hard work of the day: a dusty drag up grassy hillside on a steep shale trail.

4. At the pass turn right. (Straight is the old trail that descends very steeply to Picklejar Creek.) The preferred trail climbs up the ridge a short distance, then heads out onto the left flank and after a rocky downstep makes a downward traverse across scree into the head of Picklejar Creek. Arrive on the grassy south shore of First Lake. The encroaching scree slopes are a good place to look for picas.

Traversing meadows above Lantern Creek at 2.

Top: From where you start down to the lakes at 4 is this view of Picklejar Creek. In the distance is Mist Mountain.

Centre: The scree trail down to First Lake.

Bottom: Looking back up the trail on the return.

5. The trail continues along the grassy shoreline and across a fan of scree, then climbs into trees. On the ascent keep left, left and right. On the descent to Second Lake keep right.

6. The trail runs along the right shore in the trees. There are two ways on to third and fourth lakes. Why not make a circuit?

7. Keep straight at a junction. (To right is your return route.) The trail continues to the end of the lake then climbs, curving right below a small open hill to the north shore of Third Lake. Turn left and follow rocks around the shoreline to the east end. Here the trail climbs onto a grassy ridge then descends to Fourth Lake.

8. On the return, climb back to the grassy ridge and turn left. The high point of the grass at the edge of scree slopes is a fine viewpoint for Third and Fourth lakes.

9. From here a trail descends a little scree gully, then traverses the left (south) shore of Third Lake on rocks and scree.

10. At the west end, the trail gets lost among rocks. Keep heading west and you will pick it up again in bits of meadow. In a meadow draw it curves right and down to Second Lake.

11. Turn left and return the same way you came up.

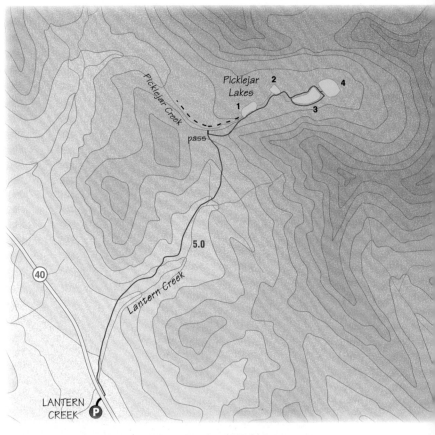

First Lake, showing its translucent green colour. This is the best lake for fishing. "The fishing is so good it's like catching fish in a picklejar," or so the saying goes.

Right: Second Lake is pale green and has a surround of drowned trees. It connects to First Lake via a short-lived but boisterous creek.

Below: Third Lake is blue, deep and entirely surrounded by rock. This photo is taken from the south shore trail when the water was low in the fall.

Fourth Lake is very shallow and coloured a pale orange. A spring on the north shore keeps it constantly supplied with water. In this view you are looking southeast to the head of the Picklejar cirque.

24 *Mount Burke*

Distance 12 km return
Height gain 884 m
High point 2542 m
Strenuous
Summer, fall

The old Cameron Lookout on top of Mt. Burke is one of K Country's finest viewpoints. The pack trail, built along the southwest ridge is one of K Country's most exciting routes.

Start: Hwy. 940 (Forestry Trunk Road) at Cataract Creek campground access road. A few metres after crossing Plateau Creek and before the campground entrance turn right into a small parking lot.

Difficulty: In the valley bottoms the trail varies from poor to good with a few sections of stoney creekbed which may require route finding. Possible minor creek crossings after rain. On the mountain the trail is well-marked with cairns. Below treeline are many switchbacks at a moderate grade. Above treeline the footing is shale, scree and rock. A short rock ridge may intimidate novice hikers.

NOTE The original start along an exploration road has in part been decimated by floods. Besides which, it required two wadings of Plateau Creek. Consequently it has been superseded by the trail along the north bank which is still in the process of being discovered.

1. From the parking lot head out into the meadow on a single track trail. On reaching Plateau Creek, the trail rounds a bend on stones below a high bank. On the other side the trail splits. Go either left or right. Both routes are marked by small cairns and sooner or later both climb onto the bank top. The trail follows the edge of the bank for some distance, then cuts through forest to a cairned T-junction with the exploration road in Salter Creek. Turn left. (To right the road descends to the confluence.)

2. The road heads through a narrow forested defile subject to flash floods. Occasionally the road reduces to trail, or you follow a trail winding about the disintegrating road. In all, you cross the creek 6 times, but the bed is nearly always dry. The trail is on the right bank when you spot a yellow sign reading "Mt. Burke." Turn left and cross the creek bed (cairn) and pick up a trail heading upwards.

The trail at 1 alongside Plateau Creek whose bed is continually changed by flash floods. On the topo map this creek is called Salter Creek which is obviously incorrect.

3. After a steep start you join the packhorse trail come in from the right. Keep left.

4. The trail heads to the middle of Burke's broad southwest ridge and turns sharp right. In pine forest the trail zigs back and forth 30 times at a very moderate angle, becoming steeper toward the end. Overall, treeline is reached with very little effort.

5. The trail continues up a steepish grassy slope laced with scree. The ridge has been tapering all the while and where it comes to a point is a good turnaround point for anyone put off by the view ahead. The upper part of the mountain is a wild landscape of gaudy yellow screes and rockbands.

6. The going is no more difficult than before. Continue up an easy slope, drop down a few rock steps and walk a narrow rock ridge. Horses weren't too keen on it, but it's plenty wide enough for humans.

7. On more comfortable slopes beyond, the trail carries on uphill at an easy grade, then makes a long rising traverse up the right-hand scree slope between the ridge and a rock band. High up it turns up left to the lookout which sits on the highest point of the mountain. Lacking door and windows, it makes a drafty shelter.

Above: Mt. Burke, showing the route up the southwest ridge which rises from lower right to the summit. The level section is the rock ridge.

Right: The grass slope at 5 between treeline and the rock ridge.

Above: At the top of the grass slope is this view of the upper mountain. From this angle the narrow section of the rock ridge is not visible. However, you can see the trail winding up the shale beyond the ridge.

The rock ridge at 6. Note the old telephone line that once ran all the way along the ridge to the lookout. Remnants can still be seen in the trees and on the ridge crest below the lookout.

Looking back along different parts of the rock ridge. In the distance is Cataract Creek and its cutblocks backdropped by the peaks of the High Rock Range.

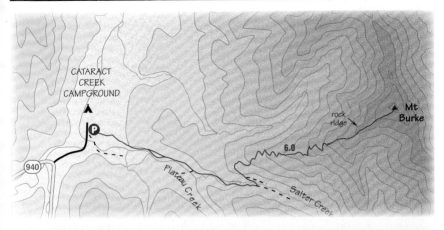

Above: At 7, the final section of trail traverses the right flank above a rock band.

Right: Cameron Lookout. Duncan Cameron ran Alberta's first weather station in 1890 in Pekisko Creek just below the mountain to the east. The mountain is named after NWMP Major Denis Burke, at one time sheriff of High River, who lived close by to Cameron in the old Francis homestead.

25 Grass Pass

Distance 6.6 km return
Height gain 427 m
High point 1875 m
Moderate
Spring, summer, fall

Start: Hwy. 541 (Highwood Trail) at Sentinel day-use area.

Difficulty: Good trail with a few moderately steep stoney sections. One minor creek crossing.

A sustained climb up Pack Trail Coulee to a grassy pass between the Bull Creek Hills and Holy Cross Mountain. If you love Limber pines, this is the walk for you.

1. Return to the highway and turn right.

2. Just past the road sign "Sentinel day-use area," turn left onto a good trail. Shortly it circles uphill to the right and joins a track at a T-junction. Turn left.

3. You follow this track all the way up Packtrail Coulee to the pass. For half its length it climbs wave after wave of stoney uphills through a forest of Douglas fir.

4. The track levels between wind-blasted aspens and you cross the tiny creek. Enter extensive bunch-grass meadows where the track resumes its upward climb, near the end veering left up steeper slopes to grassy Grass Pass.

5. This is the pass where four trails meet. Three are options. The track ahead leads down Wileman Creek to Flat Creek.

Above: Wind-blown Limber pines on all the ridges herabouts are a delight to the photographer. This photo was taken on the ridge between Grass and Gunnery passes.

Left: Starting up the final section of Packtrail Coulee at 4. The ridge above is Fir Creek Point.

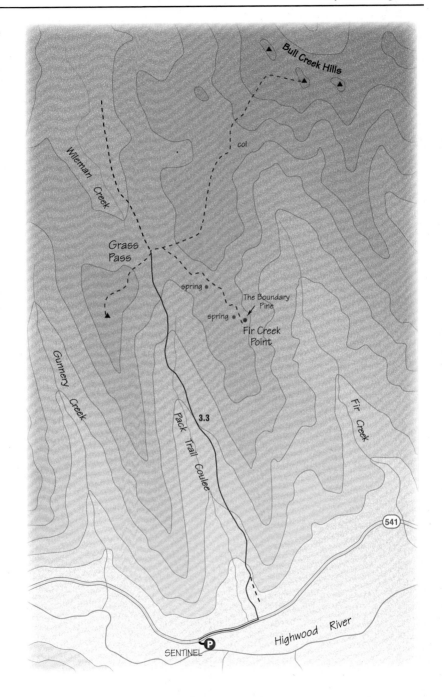

Above: Looking down Packtrail Coulee's meadows to the Highwood River valley. Across the valley the high peak is Mt. Burke.

Left: The Boundary Pine at Fir Creek Point with Grass Pass, Holy Cross Mountain and snow-covered Mt. Head in the background. The grassy ridge to left is climbed by option 3.

The Boundary Pine is a limber pine that has lost a few branches since it was made famous in R.M. Patterson's book "The Buffalo Head."

Going farther

There are three obvious possibilities, all on single track trails.

1. Fir Creek Point

Distance 1.8 km return
Height gain 80 m on return

At the pass turn right uphill, then straight-away right again. Follow a long-estab-lished cattle trail across meadows and past springs to Fir Creek Point, which is located on a south ridge descending from the Bull Creek Hills. Of most interest is the celebrated Boundary Pine.

2. Bull Creek Hills

Distance 4 km return
Height gain 265 m
High point 2134 m

At the pass turn right, then keep straight, climbing up the hill. Just before reaching the ridgetop, the trail turns left and tra-verses, descending slightly, to a col in the trees. From here climb the upper slopes of the ridge, the going straightforward on meadows dotted with limber pines. At the top bear right to a summit, which though not the highest point is a satisfy-ing viewpoint for Holy Cross Mountain and Mt. Head.

3. Ridge between Grass and Gunnery passes

Distance 1.2 km return
Height gain 85 m
High point 1900 m

At the pass turn left and climb to an open ridge where you can wander at will, en-joying the limber pines and the fabulous views in all directions.

Relaxing on the open ridge between Grass and Gunnery passes. Mt. Head in the background.

On the way up the Bull Creek Hills you look across Wileman Creek at Mt. Head (seen here) and Holy Cross Mountain to its left.

26 *Foran Grade Loop*

Distance 7.4 km loop
Height gain 280 m
High point 1686 m
Moderate
Late spring, summer, fall

In its short distance this popular loop takes in a scenic traverse above the Sheep River, a pass and an easy ridge. An excellent choice for the novice hiker.

Start: Hwy. 546 (Sheep River Trail). 1.6 km west of the winter gate at Sandy McNabb Recreation Area is a pull-out on the right side of the road. This section of Highway 546 opens May 15.

Difficulty: Good well-marked trails with occasional short moderate hills.

1. From the parking area cross the highway. A short connector trail leads to Sheep Trail at a T-junction (no sign). Turn right.

2. Descend a big meadow onto a terrace, at the bottom turning right. Enter aspen forest not far below Hwy. 546 and embark on an enjoyable traverse through aspen meadows above the Sheep River. Care is needed where the side slope steepens and there are cliffs below you. Ahead rises shapely

Windy Point Ridge. Descend to a T-junction with signpost. Go straight on Windy Point Trail. (To left Sheep Trail winds down to the Sheep River and crosses it.)

3. Windy Point Trail climbs into meadows about the Windy Point stretch of highway. Nearby is a parking lot and a couple of benches inviting you to stop and take in view looking up the Sheep River.

4. The trail crosses the highway and continues alongside Swamsons Draw. You climb in short bursts of uphills to the big flat meadow at the valley head. The pass between Windy Point and Foran Grade

Sheep Trail where it traverses above the Sheep River at 2. Ahead rises Windy Point Ridge, another popular hike, though mostly without a trail. The route follows the left-hand skyline.

ridges is reached at a T-junction. Turn right onto Foran Grade Trail. (Straight on, Windy Point Trail descends into Death Valley where it connects with the Death Valley trails.)

5. Foran Grade Trail zigs up the west slope of Foran Grade Ridge to its high point, then descends the easy-angled south ridge. Though treed, there are many clearings allowing fine views to the west and south.

6. Low down, the trail turns down the left (east) flank and in a couple of zigs reaches a very large meadow. Head down the meadow to a gate in a fence. A short stretch in pine forest brings you to the parking area on Hwy. 546.

At 2, Sheep Trail descends the big meadow below the highway.

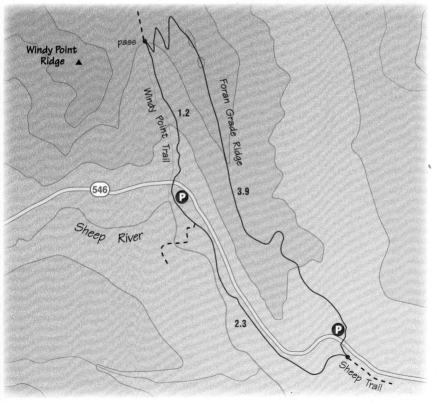

Springtime on the pass between Windy Point and Foran Grade ridges.
The photo taken from the start of the climb up to Foran Grade at 5.

View from Foran Grade Ridge of the Sheep River and Hwy. 546 winding westwards to the
Front Ranges. Two easily identifiable peaks are Gibraltar Mountain and Bluerock Mountain.

27 *Volcano Ridge Loop*

Distance 13.5 km
Height gain clockwise 380 m
High point 1905 m
Moderately strenuous
Late spring, summer, fall

A good workout through typical foothills country. On the way round who can resist climbing Volcano Ridge for its 360 degree view?

Start: Gorge Creek (road). From Hwy. 546 (Sheep River Trail) follow Gorge Creek Trail to Gorge Creek trailhead. Both roads open May 16.

Difficulty: Well-marked trails with grades varying from easy to moderately steep. Some shale and loose rocks underfoot. Minor creek crossings, sometimes bridged.

NOTE If and when Gorge Creek Trail (road) opens to Volcano Ridge trailhead, a smaller loop of 10.5 km can be made which is best hiked in an anti-clockwise direction. Alternately, many hikers prefer to make Volcano Ridge a there and back destination, a return distance of 12 km with a height gain of 366 m.

1. Head out on Gorge Creek Trail (exploration road) that descends into aspen meadows above Gorge Creek. Curve up right and cross a grassy ridge. At this point listen for the north fork cascade down below you to the left. The trail then descends to the north fork and bridges it. Walk up the left bank to a T-junction. Keep straight on Gorge Link Trail. (To left the exploration road continues up Gorge Creek.)

2. The trail heads north through extensive meadows, crossing the creek or its forks five times. Just after the fifth crossing is a T-junction. Turn left onto Volcano Ridge Trail. (Ahead is Gorge Link continued.)

3. You continue to follow the right bank of the north fork a way, then come to a fork. Cross the righthand fork and travel up the lefthand fork a short way. Cross it twice and start up a long shaley ridge under the pines. The going is relentless, with

The north fork cascade at low water. It is most easily reached by a steep trail leaving Gorge Creek Trail at the grassy ridge.

moderately steep sections. At the top you traverse above the infant north fork, then climb a bit more to a 4-way junction. Turn right onto Link Trail. (To left is a cutline; the trail ahead is Volcano Ridge Trail.)

4. Link Trail heads east on an undulating cutline. To your left across the infant Volcano Creek rises Volcano Ridge. Reach the Volcano Creek/Ware Creek watershed, which is a large area of meadows between the ridge and a rocky knoll on your right. At an unsigned T-junction just over the crest keep straight. (To left is Volcano Ridge Summit Trail.)

5. Beyond this junction the trail (now cutline access road) descends steep stoney hills into a west fork of Ware Creek and

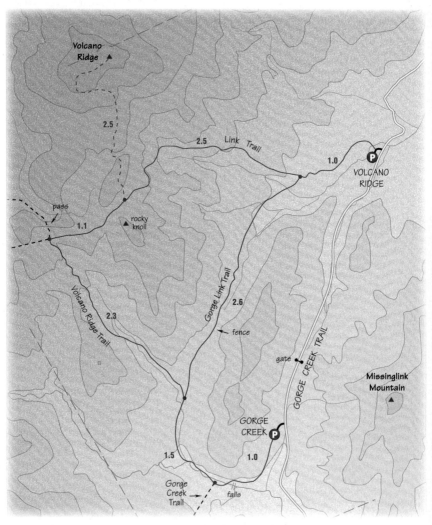

crosses it. Reverting to cutline for a way it follows the left bank, then descends further into Ware Creek valley. Come to T-junction. Turn right onto Gorge Link Trail. (Link Trail to left heads to Volcano Ridge trailhead on the highway. It follows the left bank of Ware Creek, then crosses it level with the parking lot.)

6. Gorge Link Trail crosses the west fork and follows the forested southwest fork, gaining height almost imperceptibly to the Ware Creek/Gorge Creek watershed. En route, side creek crossings are sometimes bridged. Beyond the fence marking the watershed the going is flat with a few meadows. Come to the T-junction met with earlier. Go straight, crossing the north fork of Gorge Creek, and return the same way you came up.

Right: Descending the red shales of Volcano Ridge Trail at 3. Looking towards Junction Mountain.

Below: The Volcano Creek/Ware Creek watershed from the rocky knoll at 4. Link Trail can be seen crossing the centre part of the photo from left to right. You can also spot the trail heading towards shadowy Volcano Ridge on the skyline.

The rocky knoll at 4 on the Volcano Creek/Ware Creek watershed. For many hikers climbing the knoll—actually the north end of a ridge—is an irresistible detour.

Left: Looking toward the moderately steep grassy slope from O1. You can see the trail climbing up the right side of it. The summit can just be seen at top right.

Below: A windy day on the summit.

Detour to Volcano Ridge

Distance add 5 km return
Height gain add 244 m
High point 2121 m

A favourite side trip to a superb viewpoint for Calgary and the Front Ranges. A good trail with one moderately steep hill. The last bit to the summit is over grass and shale.

1. The trail (cutline access road) follows a broad lightly treed ridge, first on the right side, then on the left, to the foot of a moderately steep grassy slope facing south.

2. The trail tackles the slope direct then contours left and around right onto the west slope. Where "the road" appears to peter out on shale, cut up right to the summit.

28 *Elbow Valley/Riverview Loop*

Distance 8.7 km loop
Height gain 240 m
High point 1622 m
Fairly easy
Spring, summer, fall

Start: Hwy. 66 (Elbow Falls Trail) at Paddy's Flat campground access road. Turn left onto the campground access road and keep straight (gated group campground to left). The road bends right into a straight, and just before it bends left is a parking lot on the left side. When the campground is closed park at the gate near the hwy.

If camped at Paddy's Flat use a trail that starts from the junction of B/C and D/E campground roads. The trail is signed "Elbow Valley Trail" and it leads to Hwy. 66 at the access road.

Difficulty: Good well-marked trails with stop signs at road crossings. Fairly easy grades with a few moderate hills.

Climbing through Lodgepole pine forest en route to the hilltop at 2. Dry open forest is typical of south and west-facing slopes in the foothills.

A rolling tour through meadows and pine forests over a hilltop and back by a river.

1. Walk back along the access road to Hwy. 66. From the far side a trail heads up right to a T-junction. Turn left onto Elbow Valley Trail. (To right the trail leads to Station Flats trailhead.)

2. Climb along a forested ridge parallel to the highway, then at a meadow turn away right, climbing through pine forest and meadow to a hilltop. In pines the trail undulates along the summit ridge to the west top, then descends grassy south slopes to a little valley. Jump the creek and climb up to Moose Mountain Road. Cross the road 1 km in from Hwy. 66.

3. Continue climbing onto Moose Mountain's southeast ridge, then wander along a terrace (two short downhills) in aspen meadows. Below open slopes come to a 4-way junction. Turn left onto Riverview Trail. (To right is Sulphur Springs Trail; ahead is Elbow Valley Trail continuing on to Canyon Creek.)

113

4. Riverview Trail descends aspen hillsides to Hwy. 66 and crosses it.

5. Continue to the top of a high bank overlooking the Elbow River. To your right the river emerges in rapids from the gorge below Canyon Creek. The trail turns left and runs along the gradually descending bank top, en route crossing a cutline. When opposite the confluence with Silvester Creek numerous side trails drop down to the river. Cross another cutline then follow a forested terrace to an unsigned T-junction identified by two steel culverts. Turn right onto Paddy's Flat Interpretive Trail. (Trail to left leads to D/E loops and the upper leg of the interpretive trail.)

6. Descend the hill to the Elbow River and turn left. (The trail to right heads upstream towards Silvester Creek and is worth a detour if you have the time.) The lower leg of the interpretive trail runs past rapids, deep pools and little sandy bays crammed with happy campers. Both the social scene and the river have quieted down by the time the trail makes a left turn across a bridge and climbs a bank. At a T-junction, keep straight. (Trail to left is the upper leg of the interpretive trail. From it are offshoots to C loop, the amphitheatre and D loop.)

7. Wind up a hill, en route touching the end of B loop, to A loop. Turn left on the campground road and walk out to the main access road. Turn right and keep straight. (To right is the upper leg of A loop.) The road turns right and you arrive back at the parking lot.

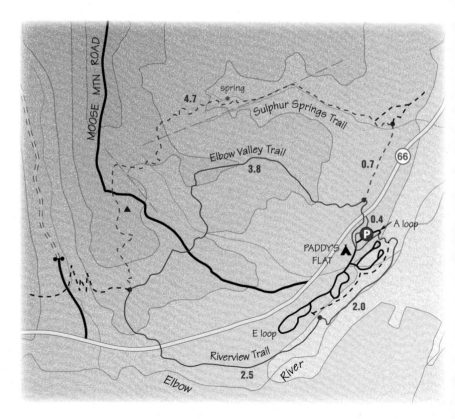

Elbow Valley Trail at 2. From the meadow on the way up the hill, you get this view of Prairie Mountain to the west.

Riverview Trail at 5. Looking down at the Elbow River from high banks. In the background are the hills about McLean Creek.

The Elbow River at 6. Below Paddy's Flat campground is a lovely stretch of rapids and deep pools.

*Left: Descending
the broad southeast
ridge at O5.*

Longer loop using Sulphur Springs Trail

Distance loop 10 km with Elbow Valley Trail,
10.3 km with Riverview Trail
Height gain 310 m with Elbow Valley Trail,
230 m with Riverview Trail

A slightly more strenuous forest trail with
one memorable viewpoint. Make loops with
either Elbow Valley Trail or Riverview Trail.

1. At the T-Junction with Elbow Valley
trail just above Hwy. 66 turn right.

2. The trail follows a forested ridge down
to Sulphur Springs Creek bridge. On the
far bank turn left onto Sulphur Springs
Trail which is a cutline access road. (The
trail ahead is Elbow Valley Trail to Station Flats.)

3. Keep straight at an unmarked junction
and undulate along the right bank of the
creek to a T-junction with a cutline. Turn
left and follow the cutline a short way.
Cross Sulphur Springs Creek and turn
right onto a trail.

4. The trail heads along the left bank of
the creek, then keaving the creek behind,
winds uphill and left. Cross the same
cutline met with earlier and the grassy

swath of a reclaimed well road. The trail
dips to a tiny creek, then climbs and crosses another cutline. Shortly after come to
Moose Mountain Road. Cross.

5. Straightaway the trail climbs to a small
"top" on Moose Mountain's southeast
ridge, then winds down a grassy slope
offering views for the first time. At the
bottom of the hill is a 4-way junction
with Elbow Valley Trail (left, right) and
Riverview Trail (straight).

The springs pouring out of a well casing.

29 *Moose Mountain*

Distance 13.8 km return
Height gain 593 m
High point 2437 m
Moderately strenuous
Late spring, summer, fall

A busy trail to a fire lookout atop Moose Mountain—alias Brokeback Mountain in the movie of the same name.

Start: Hwy. 66 (Elbow Falls Trail). 700 m west of Paddy's Flat campground access road, turn right onto the signed Moose Mountain Road. Drive past a gate (occasionally manned) and up the road that is gravelled, winding and rather steep, but well maintained. Drive for 7.3 km to a parking lot on the right side just before a gate to gas wells.

Difficulty: Good well-marked trail (fire road, then pack trail) with moderate grades. Above treeline you're walking mainly on scree, shale and rocks, sometimes above steep side slopes. Though not particularly strenuous, the trip is long and features an uphill climb on the return. Be alert for bad weather moving in. Moose Mountain is renown for its spectacular thunderstorms.

Looking back along the fire road at 2, showing the southwest-facing meadows rising to the ridge crest.

1. From the far end of the parking lot a trail climbs to the fire road. Turn left.

2. For the first 4 km the road follows a southeast ridge, keeping just below the crest on the west flank. En route you descend a long stoney hill to an unmarked junction. Keep left on the fire road. (To right is Moosepackers Trail.) After this the road winds and climbs a little, levelling off below a grassy ridge crest. Along this stretch a cutline access road turns off to the right and a side trail climbs to the ridge top—a good half-day objective with a view. Suddenly the road turns sharp left at a notch.

3. After a preliminary uphill wind, the road heads due west into alpine meadows featured in the award-winning movie "Brokeback Mountain." A long straight precedes seven easy-angled zigs up rubble to the lower summit of Moose, a pudding-shaped top known as "The Dome."

4. As you descend the other side the main peak comes into view. Novice hikers may be put off by the exciting prospect ahead, but the way up is quite easy. At the base of the final ridge the road ends and a trail takes over. Straight off a sign indicates no bikes (!) and dogs must be leashed.

5. The trail climbs along the right flank of the east ridge, then crosses to the left flank, where it makes a long rising traverse above deepening, steepening scree slopes. Almost there, you pass below the lookout on the summit and wind around the back side so as to approach it from the easier west slope via the helipad.

6. Sign the guest book and enjoy the views and resident marmots.

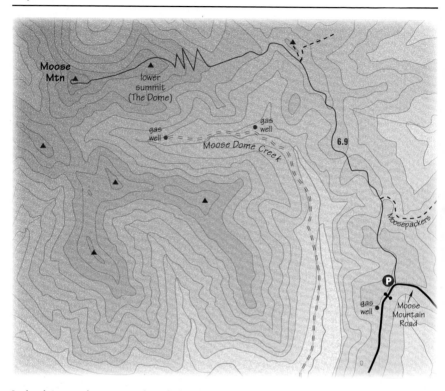

In the alpine meadows, approaching the lower summit at 3. It shows the many zigzags and shortcuts.

Above: Looking back at the lower summit from the col between the two summits. It is the apex of a major structural feature called the Moose Mountain Dome, an inlay of Paleozoic limestone rocks surrounded by sandstones of a more recent age.

Below: The main summit from The Dome at 4. The trail can be seen winding up the ridge facing.

High up at 5 the trail traverses a steep scree slope below the ridge line.

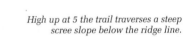

The latest lookout was built in 1974, the first in 1929. Back then horses brought supplies along the trail from Elbow Ranger Station.

The lookout is usually busy, so unless he or she comes out to greet you, don't call in to say "hello." Just sign the guest book outside.

Starting down from the summit. In the background is North Peak and the north ridge. The grassy hill at top left is Cox Hill.

30 *Prairie Mountain*

Distance 6.8 km return
Height gain 686 m
High point 2210 m
Moderately strenuous
Spring, summer, fall

Start: Hwy. 66 (Elbow Falls Trail) at Beaver Lodge parking lot located on the left side of the highway just west of the winter gate and Elbow Falls access road. When the road is closed park at the winter gate. The road opens May 16.

Difficulty: A fair to good trail with widely varying grades. Of note is the short steep start and the sustained moderately steep climb up the upper southeast ridge. In early spring and late fall expect to encounter ice on the top half of this section.

A favourite climb with locals and keep fit enthusiasts to an open summit with panoramic views.

How the trail starts off up the bank at 2.

1. Cross the highway and get onto Elbow Valley Trail heading right (east). It parallels the highway. Keep straight twice (Prairie Creek Trail to left) and cross Prairie Creek by culvert. On the east bank of the creek turn left up the unsigned Prairie Mountain Trail. (Straight ahead with the red marker is Elbow Valley Trail.)

2. To gain the southeast ridge, your ascent route, the trail climbs the steep bank overlooking the highway at its left-hand edge. The going is occasionally steep and rocky and at the mid point are interweaving strands of trail. I recommend going right at questionable junctions. Just before gaining the southeast ridge go either left or right.

3. At the top the trail steers left along a broad gently-rising section of ridge with occasional viewpoints.

4. Gradually the serious climbing begins, over 350 vertical m of corkscrewing up the forested upper ridge. At the mid point there's an easing on patches of stony ground, then the trail steepens again for the final push to the summit ridge. Emerge at treeline—the start of wind-buffeted meadows.

5. Turn right and hug the edge of the eastern escarpment around to the summit cairn 1 km distant. The view is panoramic (Calgary can be seen to the east). Closer in to the north is Moose Mountain and to its right Moose Dome Creek, site of several sour gas wells. On the cliffs above Canyon Creek look for a dark slit that is the entrance to Canyon Creek Ice Cave.

6. Anyone with energy to spare can wander the grassy northwest ridge for more views into Canyon Creek.

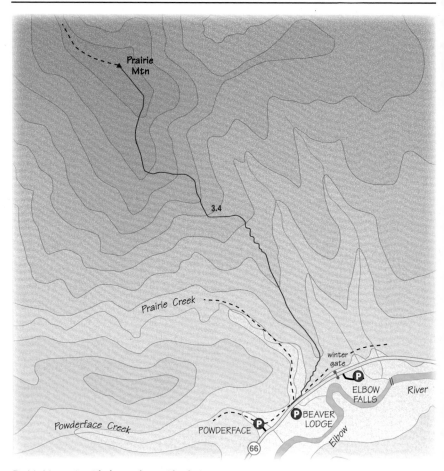

*Prairie Mountain with the southeast ridge facing.
Initially the trail follows the left-hand edge of the
open bank overlooking Hwy. 66.*

Climbing the upper slopes of the southeast ridge at 4. Photo Roy Millar.

On topping out onto the summit ridge at 5 you walk the edge of the eastern escarpment around to the summit meadows.

Left: Higher up at 5 the meadows are exposed to strong westerly winds.

Centre: The always leaning branch in the summit cairn. Looking west to summits of the Fisher Range.

Moose Mountain arises above satellite peaks that are not often climbed. The Stoneys call the whole massif Iyarhe Wida, meaning "mountain by itself." To the left you can just see the tip of the northwest ridge.

31 *Powderface Ridge*

Distance 10 km
Height gain 594 m
High point 2210 m
Moderately strenuous
Late spring, summer, fall

A long approach through forest and over two cols to a grassy ridge top. With two vehicles there is the option of prolonging the meadow walk.

Start: At the junction of Hwy. 66 (Elbow Falls Trail) and Powderface Trail (road) is a small parking area on the north side. If full, use a parking area 200 m along Hwy. 66 toward Little Elbow Recreation Area. Both roads open May 16.

Difficulty: A good well-marked trail with two long climbs at a moderate grade. You share the trail with mountain bikers who will be descending your ascent route.

1. From the usual parking area a trail climbs the bank to a junction. Turn right. (To left is a trail come in from Forgetmenot Pond.)

2. The trail delves into pine forest and climbs a moderately angled ridge into meadows about col no. 1. If you have time it's worth walking out to the grassy outlier at right for the breathtaking view to the southwest.

3. After a stint through trees, the trail rises through even lusher meadows to col no. 2 with a cairn. To right rises a knoll at the end of Rainy Pass Ridge. Although it lacks the view to the west, it is nevertheless a popular objective for people ready to call it quits.

4. The trail enters damp mossy spruce forest on the east flank of the ridge. The trend is downhill. Cross two tiny creeks, the first with piper water! After the crossings you're into the second big climb of the day—an ascending traverse with wave after wave of uphills. A cairn signals the last lap, three zigs up onto the ridge crest. You break through the rocky escarpment into meadows and turn right. A few metres along, the highest point of the trail is marked with a cairn and a post. To the west is a stunning view of Nihahi Ridge.

Powderface Ridge from the south. This view shows the route up the forested spur at middle left to the grassy col at centre and on to a second grassy col at centre right. To the right of the second col rises a knoll where some people call it a day. The summit is seen through the gap.

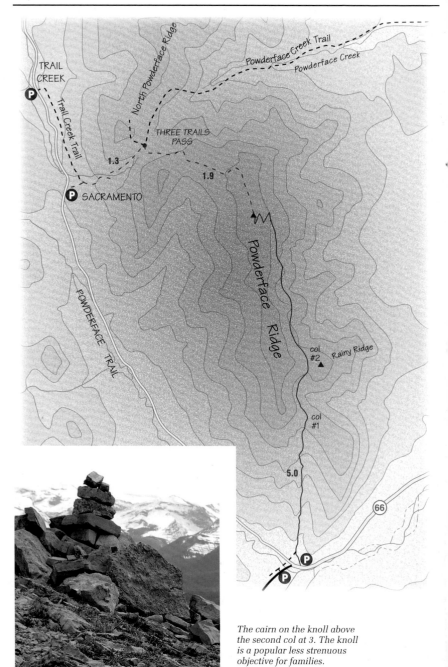

The cairn on the knoll above the second col at 3. The knoll is a popular less strenuous objective for families.

Right: Approaching the second col through lush meadows at 3.

Centre: A cool cloudy day on the summit of Powderface Ridge. Looking northwest toward the north end of Nihahi Ridge. In the middle ground is the grass ridge from where the next photo was taken.

Bottom: Powderface Ridge from the ridge to the west. It shows the optional descent route from the summit down to the col at middle left (O1) from where it drops off into Three Trail Pass.

Nearing Three Trail Pass at O2. Behind is North Powderface Ridge and Moose Mountain.

The trail at O3 leading down through a matchstick pine forest.

Optional descent to Sacramento Pass via Three Trail Pass

Distance 3.2 km
Height loss 366 m

With two vehicles hikers can continue walking the meadows down to Three Trail Pass and out via Trail Creek Trail to Powderface Trail (road) at Sacramento Pass, which is the first pass you encounter if you drive north on Powderface Trail (road) from the junction with Hwy. 66. While there is no designated parking area at the pass, there is room off road for a couple of vehicles.

The trail is well-marked and grades remain moderate with good footing.

1. On trail continue north along the grassy ridge top. All too soon the trail veers to the left (west) and descends a broad slope dotted with krummholz to the col between the ridge and its western outlier.

2. Here the trail turns right and descends very gradually through trees, low down turning right into the meadows about Three Trail Pass (also known as Powderface Pass). Come to a 4-way junction with signpost. Turn left onto Trail Creek Trail. (To right is Powderface Creek Trail. Straight on is an unsigned trail leading onto North Powderface Ridge.)

3. The Trail Creek Trail descends shaley meadows into pine forest alongside a creek. Cross the creek and continue down through a matchstick pine forest. At an unsigned junction keep left on a very obvious old road. (To right Trail Creek Trail re-crosses the creek en route to Trail Creek trailhead on Powderface Trail (road).)

4. In short order the old road reaches Powderface Trail (road) at Sacramento Pass, which is named after a long-standing rain gauge at the site.

32 *Nihahi Ridge*

Distance 5.6 km return to viewpoint
Height gain 365 m
High point 1981 m
Moderate
Late spring, summer, fall

Start: Hwy. 66 (Elbow Falls Trail) at Little Elbow Recreation Area. Just before the campground gate turn left into a very large parking lot signed "Trailhead Parking." Park at the far end beyond the biffy. Hwy. opens May 16.

Difficulty: Good well-marked trail with occasional steep grades. Near trail's end the footing is on scree and rock.

Note: Lucky campers can walk to the hunter's parking lot at 7 and pick up the trail there. Everyone else must start from the parking lot. Deduct 3.1 km return via the campground access road, 3.2 km return via Little Elbow Interpretive Trail.

A scenic meadow walk onto the lower south end of a very long ridge called Nihahi, meaning "rocky" in Stoney.

1. From the far left-hand corner of the parking lot near the biffy, get onto Little Elbow Interpretive Trail which parallels the campground access road and saves a road walk.

2. Immediately keep straight twice. (Trail to left leads to Forgetmenot Pond; trail to right cuts across to the campground access road.) At the next junction veer right.

3. Walk upstream on the right bank of the Little Elbow River towards the suspension bridge. En route, a trail joining in from the right has come from the equestrian campground. The trail rises to the level of the suspension bridge and there crosses Big Elbow Trail.

4. A little farther on, side trails come in across the road from C loop, then D loop.

Crossing the big meadow at 11 toward Nihahi Ridge. The main trail follows the ridgeline from middle left to the saddle of orange shale seen at upper right.

At 12, looking up at step no. 2 below the saddle.

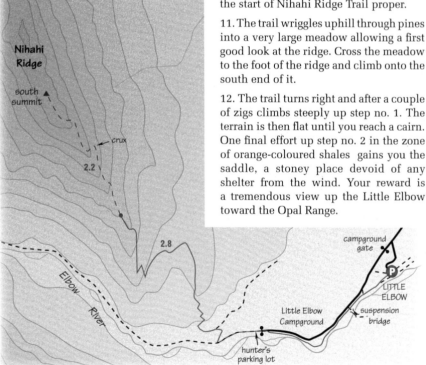

5. The trail rises to a viewpoint overlooking the Little Elbow River, then traverses the bank just below the campground access road. At an interpretive sign it joins the road opposite E loop.

6. Turn left and walk up the road to the bend on F loop.

7. Leave the campground road at the bend with kiosk. Walk through the gate and down the hill to the hunter's parking lot. Little Elbow Trail (fire road) starts from the far end of the lot.

8. Straightaway, keep straight on the fire road (grassed-over trail to your right). At a signpost turn right onto a trail.

9. Climb to a T-junction. Turn left, following a horse trail from the equestrian campground.

10. At the top of a hill turn right. This is the start of Nihahi Ridge Trail proper.

11. The trail wriggles uphill through pines into a very large meadow allowing a first good look at the ridge. Cross the meadow to the foot of the ridge and climb onto the south end of it.

12. The trail turns right and after a couple of zigs climbs steeply up step no. 1. The terrain is then flat until you reach a cairn. One final effort up step no. 2 in the zone of orange-coloured shales gains you the saddle, a stoney place devoid of any shelter from the wind. Your reward is a tremendous view up the Little Elbow toward the Opal Range.

Going farther to Nihahi Ridge South Summit

Distance 4.4 km return
Height gain 405 m
High Point 2380 m

Going to the south summit is for hikers who enjoy an easy scramble. Expect loose rock, the use of hands and a narrow ridge at the end. Pointing the way is a poor trail.

1. Continue up the scree ridge on a trail that on reaching the rock step traverses below it on the right side at the top of trees. After passing a second step, the trail zigs uphill to the ridge crest for a brief visit. A third step is avoided by a similar traverse on the right side below the cliff band and above a rubble slope. Come to where the rockband narrows.

Left: Scrambling up the crux crack at O2.

The second traverse below the third rockband at O1. The dark streak just to the right of the hiker's head is the crux crack up to the scree slopes above. The upper picture on the next page was taken from the scree "summit" at top centre.

2. Scramble up a 4 m-high, dark-looking diagonal crack plentifully supplied with holds (the crux). Often it is wet.

3. The trail continues up the easy scree above to the ridge crest, then heads right. Follow the crest a way, then traverse around to the right and back left into a much steeper section of ridge that turns sharp left (west). On the left side are cliffs, but to the right is a broken slope up which the trail picks a route. A few easy scrambling moves at the top gain you the crest where the ridge resumes its northward march. Here many hikers congregate, then decide to go down.

4. Admittedly the ridge rising to the South Summit cairn is fairly narrow with cliffs on the right and broken slabs on the left. But by placing your feet carefully you should have no trouble.

5. From the cairn the undulating ridge continues for another 6 km, and is rated a moderate scramble.

Above: At O3, looking up the steeper section of ridge to the summit ridge and south summit at far right. The terrain is broken up and quite easy.

The final hike to the south summit at O4 is over broken slabs. As you can tell from the photo, the angle is gentle and there is no need for the use of hands.

33 *Forgetmenot Ridge*

Distance 9.2 km return north top
Height gain 625 m
High point 2240 m
Strenuous
Late spring, summer, fall

A tough climb to a favourite ridge renowned for its meadows and mountain views. Most people stop at the north top.

Start: Hwy. 66 (Elbow Falls Trail) at Little Elbow Recreation Area. Just before the campground gate turn left into a very large parking lot signed "Trailhead Parking." Park at the far end beyond the biffy. Hwy. opens May 16.

Difficulty: Good well-marked trails to the foot of the mountain. Good to poor trails to treeline with cairns. The ascent has steep grades and much scree underfoot. Possible river crossing of a channel of the Elbow River earlier in the season.

View of Forgetmenot Ridge from Ford Knoll. It shows the ascent ridge rising at centre and the north summit at left.

1. From the far left-hand corner of the parking lot near the biffy, get onto Little Elbow Interpretive Trail which parallels the campground access road and saves a road walk.

2. Immediately keep straight twice. (Trail to left leads to Forgetmenot Pond; trail to right cuts across to the campground access road.) At the next junction veer right.

3. Walk upstream on the right bank of the Little Elbow River towards the suspension bridge. The trail rises to the level of the bridge and intersects Big Elbow Trail a few metres in from the campground access road. Turn left and cross the bridge.

4. Big Elbow Trail (fire road) wends left down a hill onto the flats. At a T-junction turn right. Keep straight to a signed 4-way junction. Turn left onto Wildhorse Trail (old road). (Ahead is Big Elbow Trail; to right a horse trail.)

5. Wildhorse Trail heads toward the Elbow River, en route intersecting the equestrian trail (old road) and then a cutline. After a few windings keep right (track to left) and

Toiling up the northwest ridge at 8. Photo Tony Daffern.

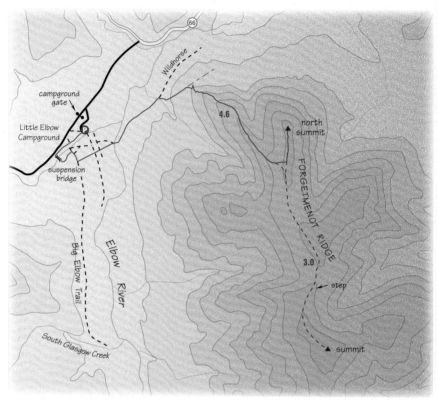

arrive at the Elbow River. At this point the water often runs underground and all you have to do is cross a wide stoney creekbed. You may encounter some water in the channel nearest the far bank.

6. Continue on road for another 1 km. Just after crossing a tiny side creek turn right onto a single-track trail at a large cairn.

7. Head along the left bank of the side creek, then turn sharp left onto a narrow cutline. What follows is a very steep climb onto the northwest ridge of Forgetmenot. Here the cutline levels. After a short rise turn right onto the ridge trail. (The cutline ahead has branches laid across it.)

8. Though never more than moderately steep, the climb up the lower northwest ridge is relentless. There are many zigs and twistings, mostly on scree. En route watch for the Holey Rock Tree which rattles in the wind! Higher up the terrain and the gradient moderate somewhat. Top out at two cairns.

9. The upper ridge is flat, the trail continuing through trees and on grass to where the ridge abuts against the main body of the mountain.

10. The trail climbs up right through last trees onto open slopes of grass and stones, then peters out. Most people just climb straight up to the summit ridge.

11. From here the north summit is just an easy walk away to your left. Look across to valley to Powderface Ridge.

The Holey Rock Tree at 8.

The gentle slope rising to the north summit at 11.

Going farther to the summit

Distance 6 km return
Height gain add 115 m
High point 2335 m

Having done all the hard work, why not enjoy the walk along the ridge to the highest summit? While there is little in the way of a trail, the route is obvious. The ridge is broad and grassy with a few rocks to hop over near the summit. Grades are easy apart from one short step of easy scrambling at the step.

1. If missing out the north summit, head up right when the trail peters out, looking for a line of cairns guiding you across stoney ground to a low point.

2. From here head southeast, rising slightly over the shoulder of an eastern top and on down to a col below "the step."

3. Here the ridge narrows and turns to the southwest. A trail on the crest leads up to the rocks which are easily scrambled up on the left side.

4. The ridge ahead is once again broad and easy-angled. Enjoy a lovely stretch through meadow strewn with rocks.

5. The ridge turns back to the southeast and once again changes character, grass alternating with rocks aligned across the ridge in wide stripes. Rock hopping is unavoidable. The summit area is flat and you have to search to find the summit cairn.

Looking toward the step and the summit from the low point at O1.

Right: Coming up to the step at 3 where the ridge turns southwest. To left is the summit.

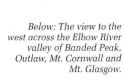

Below: The view to the west across the Elbow River valley of Banded Peak, Outlaw, Mt. Cornwall and Mt. Glasgow.

The ridge above the step at O4. Rising up in the background is the north summit.

34 *Jumpingpound Mountain*

Distance 13.8 km return
Height gain 580 m
High point 2225 m
Moderate
Late spring, summer, fall

Start: Powderface Trail (Hwy.) at Lusk Pass trailhead (no biffy). The road opens May 16 and closes November 30.

Difficulty: A well-marked trail with easy to moderate grades. In spring, deep snowbanks on the east flank may force you to clamber over the boulderfield.

This approach to Jumpingpound Mountain takes you along the lovely north ridge with its panoramic views.

1. The Jumpingpound Ridge Trail leaves from the opposite side of the road and straightaway crosses a bridge over Jumpingpound Creek.

2. Start the climb up a forested side ridge with 10 easy-angled zigs. At half height the trail straightens, flattens briefly, then resumes a twisting climb to the north ridge at treeline. At a T-junction turn right. (To left is Coxhill Ridge Trail.)

3. It's an easy walk through windswept meadows along the almost flat and wide north ridge. At a boulderfield the trail dekes into east flank trees for a spell. Back on the ridge you pass to the left of a tiny reflecting tarn. On a clear day the sheer number of peaks you can see to the west from this ridge is astonishing.

4. Below the summit—a grassy pyramid fringed with rocks on your left—is an unsigned junction. The main trail ahead crosses the west flank and misses it out. So keep left, then climb up left at a second junction. Just below the top leave the trail which continues along the east ridge and walk up a few rocks to the summit.

5. Return the same way or with two vehicles use the Optional Descent.

At the T-junction with Coxhill Ridge Trail at 2. This is the start of the north ridge seen ahead.

The meadows are not lush, but rather wind-blasted tundra. In Spring more sheltered glades are carpeted with Prairie crocus.

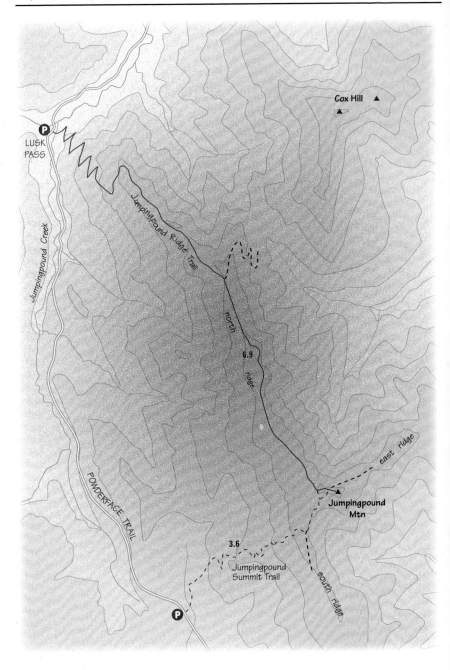

At 3, looking toward the summit that is still a few kilometres away at far left. The north ridge is characterized by 2 m-high cairns that help hikers navigate in bad weather.

The reflecting tarn with the peaks of the Fisher Range in the background.

Not far below the summit is a spectacular view looking northwest toward mounts Lougheed and Rundle on the skyline.

The summit of Jumpingpound Mountain with Moose Mountain peeping over its shoulder.

Optional descent via Jumpingpound Summit Trail

Distance 3.6 km one way
Height loss 396 m

With two vehicles, a descent can be made down Jumpingpound Summit Trail to the highway. On bad weather days, this hikers only trail is a popular ascent route to the summit, being mostly in forest. A well-marked trail with easy grades and all creeks bridged.

Finish (or start) at Powderface Trail (road) at Jumpingpound Summit parking area, 6 km south from Lusk Pass trailhead. Just over a low pass watch for a "P" sign on the right (west) side of the road.

1. Head back down the trail. At the first junction turn left. Keep left and descend into the trees of the south ridge. Come to a T-junction. Turn right onto Jumpingpound Summit Trail. (Trail ahead is Jumpingpound Ridge Trail.)

Another view of the summit looking northwest. Winter ascents via Jumpingpound Summit Trail are popular until the road closes on December 1.

2. The trail makes many easy-angled zigs down a forested west ridge. Low down cross tiny side creeks on bridges. At the bottom of the hill, the trail turns left and runs alongside a north fork of Canyon Creek. Eventually you cross the creek and walk up to the highway opposite the parking area.

35 Cox Hill

Distance 13.2 km return
Height gain 730 m
High point 2219 m
Moderately strenuous
Late spring, summer, fall

Start: Powderface Trail (Hwy.) at Lusk Pass trailhead (no biffy). The road opens May 16 and closes November 30.

Difficulty: Well-marked trails with moderate grades. A 170 m dip in the middle makes this route a more strenuous undertaking than # 34.

The south ridge meadow route up Cox Hill is much more enjoyable than the regular forest route up the north ridge. The distance is about the same.

1. The Jumpingpound Ridge Trail leaves from the opposite side of the road and straightaway crosses a bridge over Jumpingpound Creek.

2. Start the climb up a forested side ridge with 10 easy-angled zigs. At half height the trail straightens, flattens briefly, then resumes a twisting climb to the north ridge at treeline. At a T-junction turn left onto Coxhill Ridge Trail. (To right is Jumpingpound Ridge Trail.)

3. The trail traverses along then starts its descent to the Jumpingpound/Cox col. A third of the way down a shale shoulder gives a view of Cox Hill ahead. Below this the trail picks a way down between small crags, then in trees makes a long down-

The shale shoulder at 3. Looking toward the south ridge of Cox Hill.

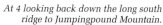

At 4 looking back down the long south ridge to Jumpingpound Mountain.

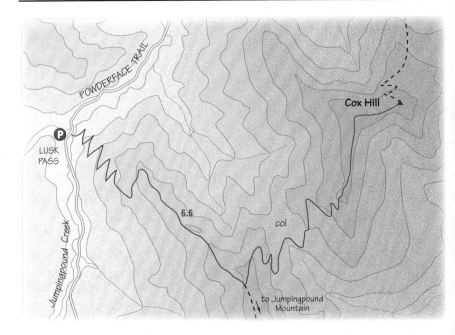

ward sweep to the left. Near the bottom turn right and reach the col.

4. To attain the south ridge of Cox, the trail uses a western side ridge. Getting on to it is the steepest climb of the day through meadow and trees and over rocks. Once on the ridge and heading up it the climb is much more gradual.

5. Near treeline a left turn sets you on a very long rising traverse out of the trees along the west flank of the south ridge. The going is easy on dry shaley meadow.

6. Suddenly the trail turns up right to the summit cairn. On two sides Cox is fringed with rockbands that make great grandstand seats for viewing the mountain panorama.

7. It's worth carrying on along the summit ridge (a few trees) to the grassy eastern summit for new views to the north and east. Coming up from the left is the north ridge trail from Dawson day-use area.

The summit rocks at 6. Originally the hill was named Cockscomb after these rocks.

A chance meeting with friends on the summit. Looking east to Moose Mountain and the east ridge of Jumpingpound Mountain.

The main summit from the east summit cairn at 7. The slope down right was the scene of a tragic plane crash in 1986.

Phone Numbers and E-mail Addresses

- Kananaskis Country trail report: 1-403-678-3136. www.cd.gov.ab.ca/enjoying_alberta/parks/featured/kananaskis/trailreport.aspx.

- Bear and cougar sightings: For an up to date list of sightings in the Bow Valley area: www.trailex.org. See also www.bvwildsmart.ca.

- Barrier Lake Information Centre 1-403-673-3985.

- Peter Lougheed Provincial Park Information Centre 1-403-591-6322.

- Elbow Valley Information Centre 1-403-949-4261.

- Sheep River Provincial Park Office 1-403-933-7172.

- Mount Engadine Lodge 1-403-678-4080. www.mountengadine.com.

- The hotels at Kananaskis Village: Delta Lodge 1-888-432-4322, Executive Resort 1-403-591-7500.

- Rafter Six Ranch Resort: 1-888-26RANCH. Local: 1-403-673-3622. reservations@raftersix.com. www.raftersix.com.

- Sundance Lodges 1-403-591-7122.

> ### EMERGENCY
> Dial 911 and ask for
> Kananaskis Dispatch

Campground Information

For Hwy. 1X, Hwy. 1, Hwy. 68
Bow Valley Park Campgrounds
1-403-673-2163.
www.bowvalleycampgrounds.com.

For Hwy. 66, Hwy. 546, Hwy. 66
Kananaskis Country Campgrounds
1-403-949-3132.
www.kananaskiscountrycampgrounds.com.

For Peter Lougheed Provincial Park, Hwy. 742, Hwy. 40
Kananaskis Country Campgrounds
1-866-366-2267. Local: 1-403-591-7226.
www.kananaskiscountrycampgrounds.com.

For Mt. Kidd RV Park on Hwy. 40
1-403-591-7700.

Acknowledgments

The following provided photos as credited in the text: Jim Bell, Allan Cole, Tony Daffern, Rob Laird, John Martin, Roy Millar, Chic Scott, Peter Snell, David Wasserman. Thank you everybody for your generosity in sharing your pictures.